AF321527

# IN SUSSEX

Published in 2022
by Unicorn, an imprint of Unicorn Publishing Group LLP
5 Newburgh Street, London W1F 7RG
www.unicornpublishing.org



ISBN 978-1-914414-38-1
10 9 8 7 6 5 4 3 2 1

Designed by Felicity Price-Smith

# IN SUSSEX
## BOB MAZZER

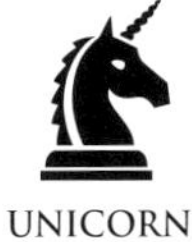

UNICORN

## Bob Mazzer by Eamonn McCabe

When I first saw the cover of Bob Mazzer's last book it frightened the life out of me. There was this huge guy, shirtless, with an enormous lizard clinging to one shoulder and with Bob Mazzer in large capital letters emblazoned across his chest. I could never have taken his picture – let alone write a foreword to his new book – in case he decked me if he didn't like it.

At least I thought it was Bob, but it turned out to be just one of his wonderful photographs taken on a beach on the south coast. Bob himself, as it turns out, is a very gentle observer of life in St Leonards, Sussex where he now lives and works. I need not have worried. It turns out that we have been close to each other over the years without actually knowing each other.

I was in California in 1969 when Bob, who (like me) loves his hats, was also in the United States, when we were both twenty-one. I lived in Manor House, north London at the same time that Bob was working in a porn cinema in King's Cross as a projectionist, where I did some work for *Time Out* just around the corner, as did Bob in his spare time. We must have often been on the Tube at the same time.

It was at Woodberry Down Comprehensive School that the photographer Euan Duff opened Bob's eyes to the possibilities and history of photography.

The Sussex photographs are mainly in black and white, which Bob loves, and are of people close to the edge where he feels some affinity. Apart from some beautiful landscapes, Bob would never have got a shift with the local tourist board. Most of his subjects have struggled in their life, but often with a smile on their face; real people living real lives.

Bob loves meeting people on the street in his own neighbourhood and says it is a kind of therapy: 'You look all over the world and then you find what you are looking for in your own back yard.'

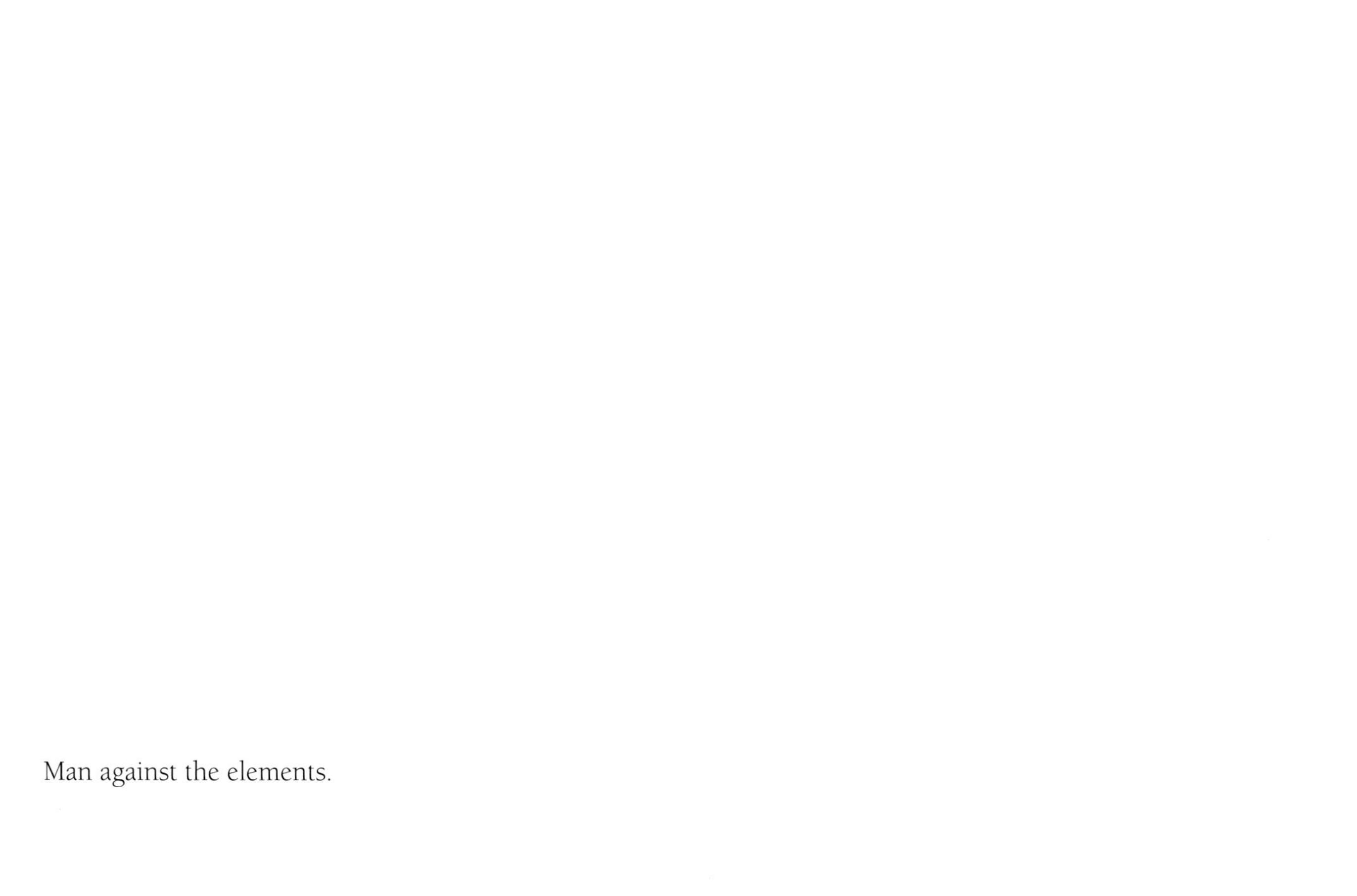

Man against the elements.

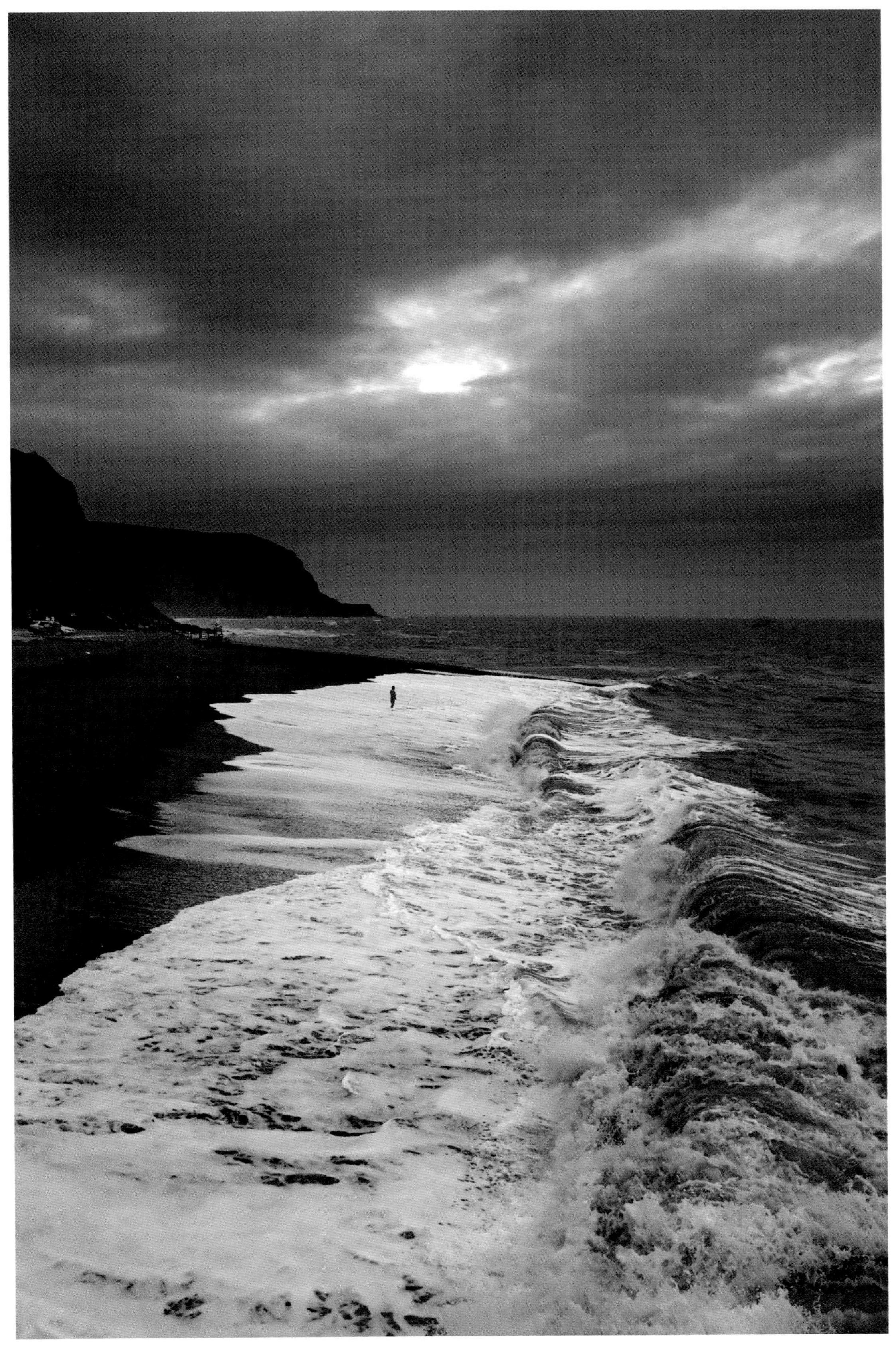

A Covid outing – Jen and me getting away from all the
mess. Throwing our masks on the back seat of the car
and just driving. It was a relief to be out and about.
Really good therapy. Perfect days.

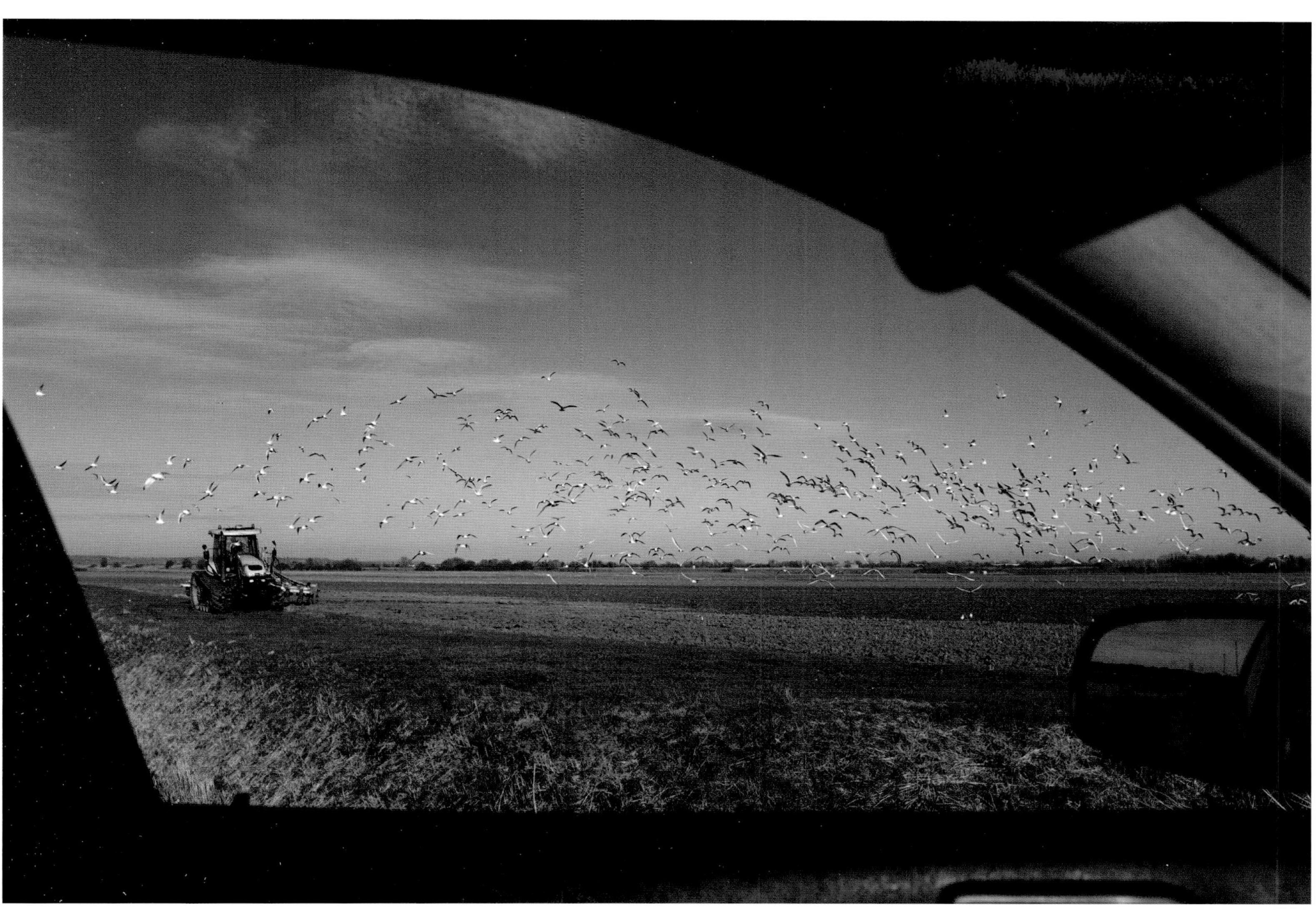

Another Covid journey. An endless, lovely voyage
of discovery. Big and expansive countryside – always
something new around the corner. It allowed Jen
and me to release the gypsy in us.

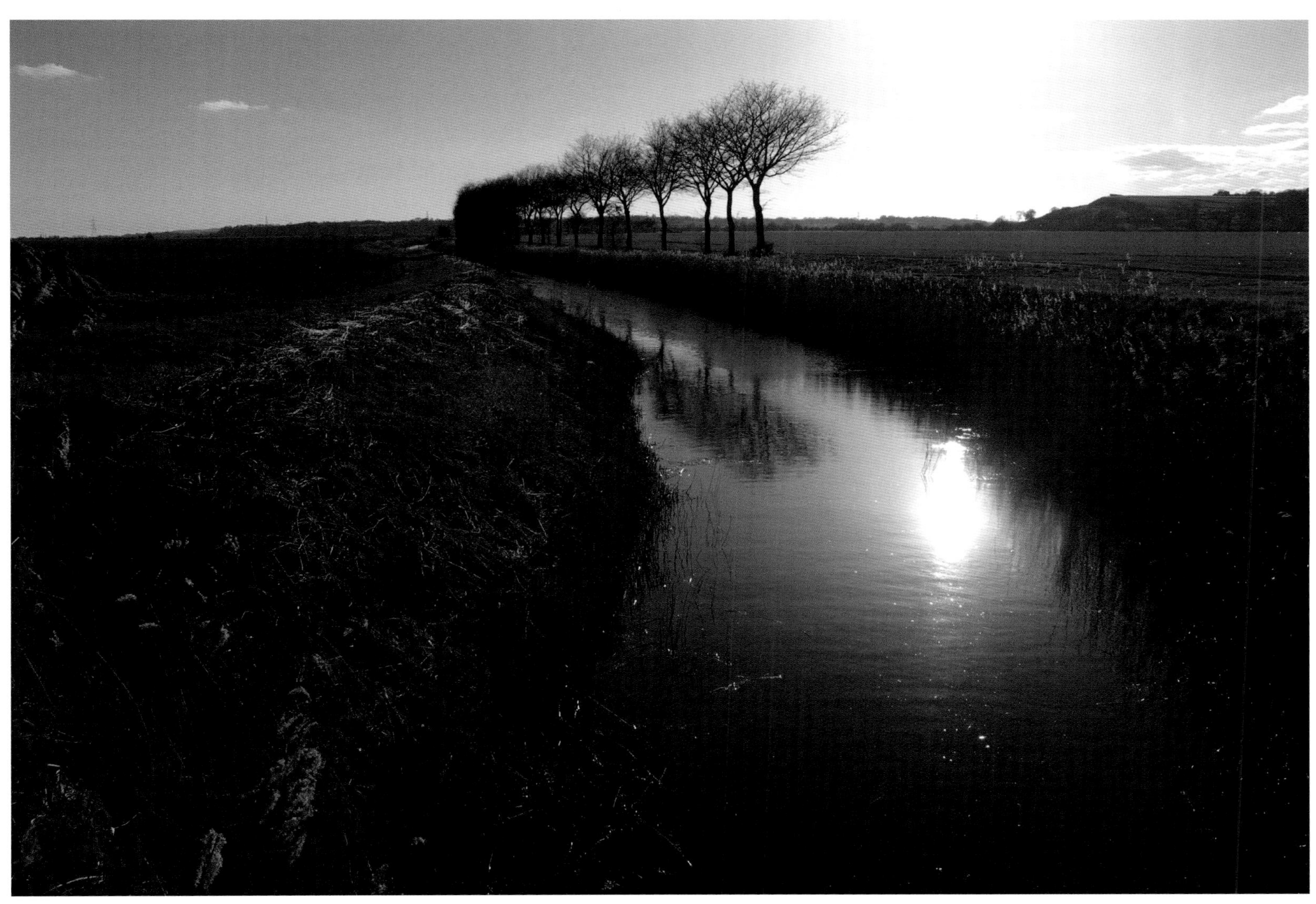

This is the other end of Camber Sands where they have
built this huge sea defence. It looks like a massive sci-fi
scene.

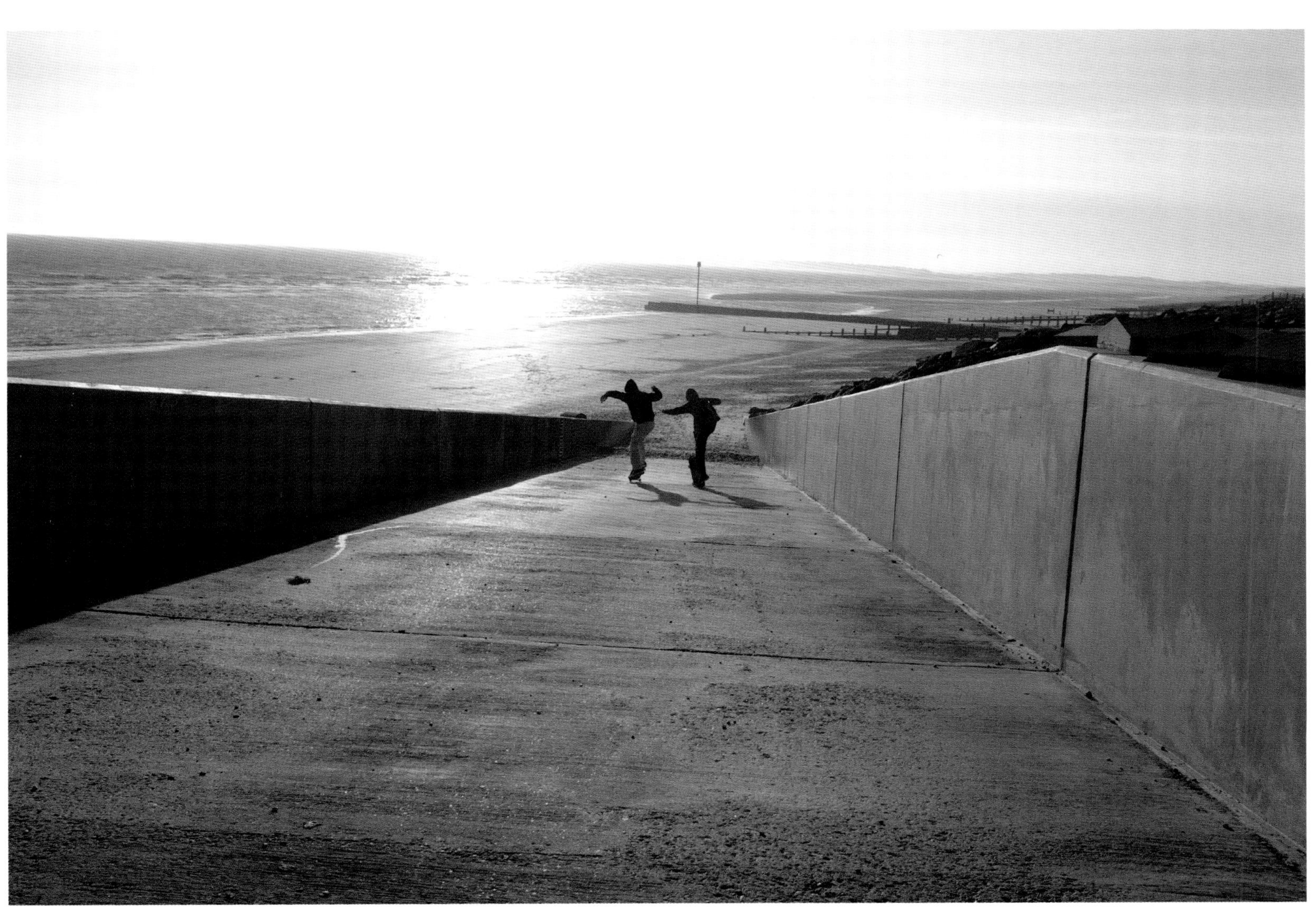

Hastings' Bonfire Night.
I took many pictures that night, but none of the
actual bonfire. Always of people, slightly left of field;
the quieter moments.

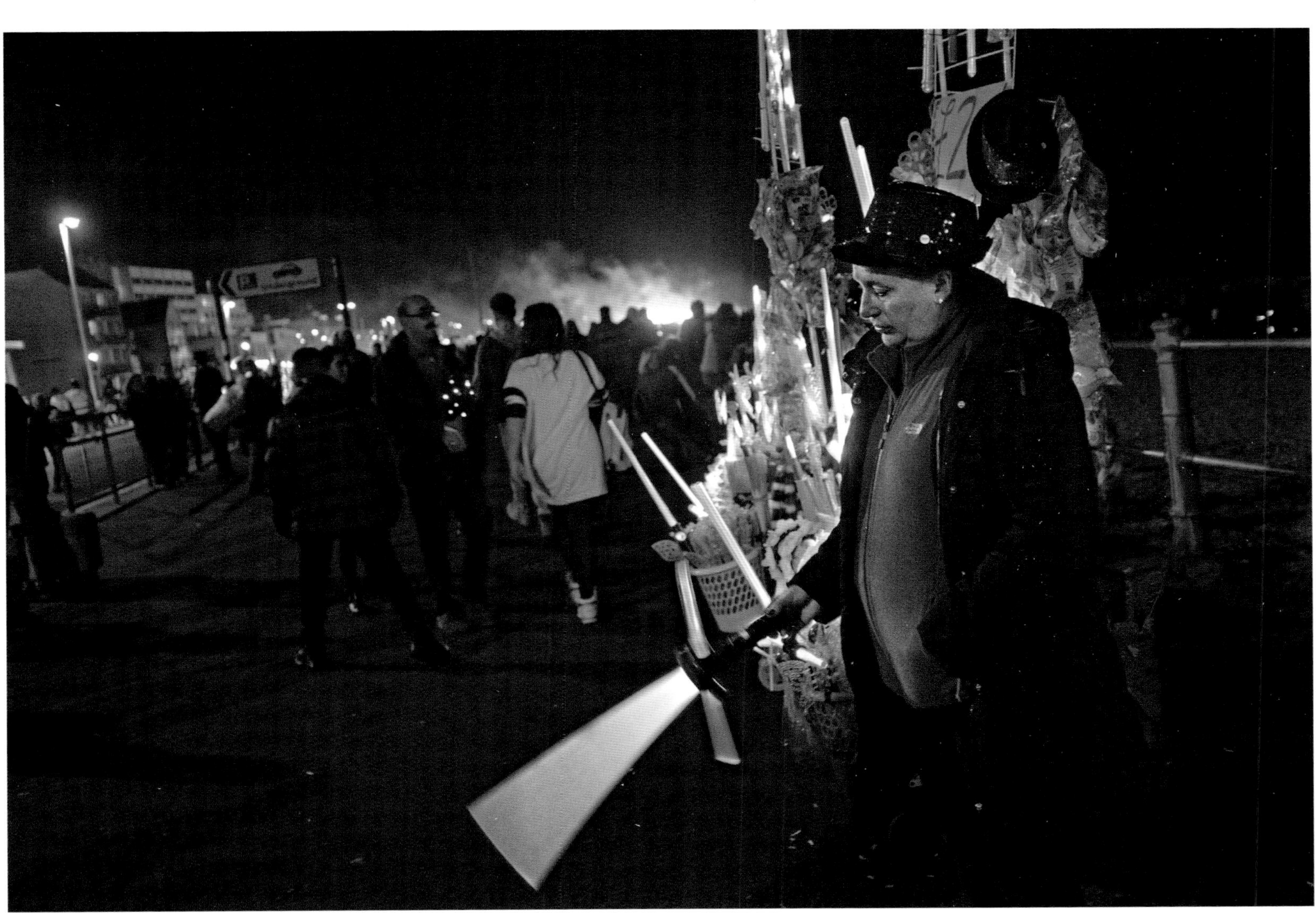

Standing on the end of the pier, did I notice them
earlier? They looked interesting so I deliberately
ignored them, by standing right in front of them.
I knew I only had one chance at taking this shot.
I knew they were sad about something. You could
tell even from the back. When I'd worked it all out
– the aperture, the shutter speed, the camera
business – I swung around and clicked.

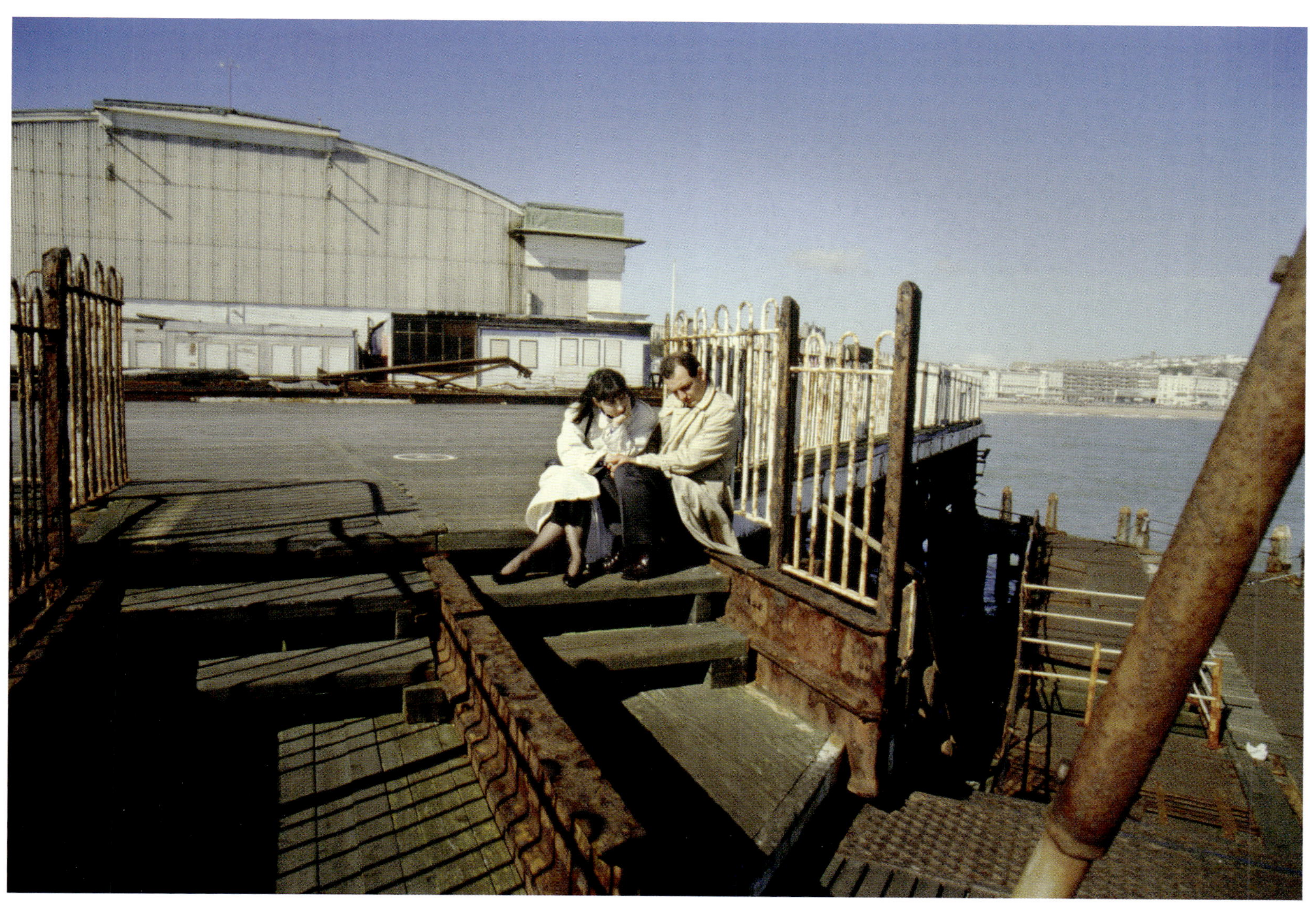

When I first exhibited this photo, I was asked
to take it down on sensitive grounds. Hopefully
over twenty years later, the girls are less
recogniseable.

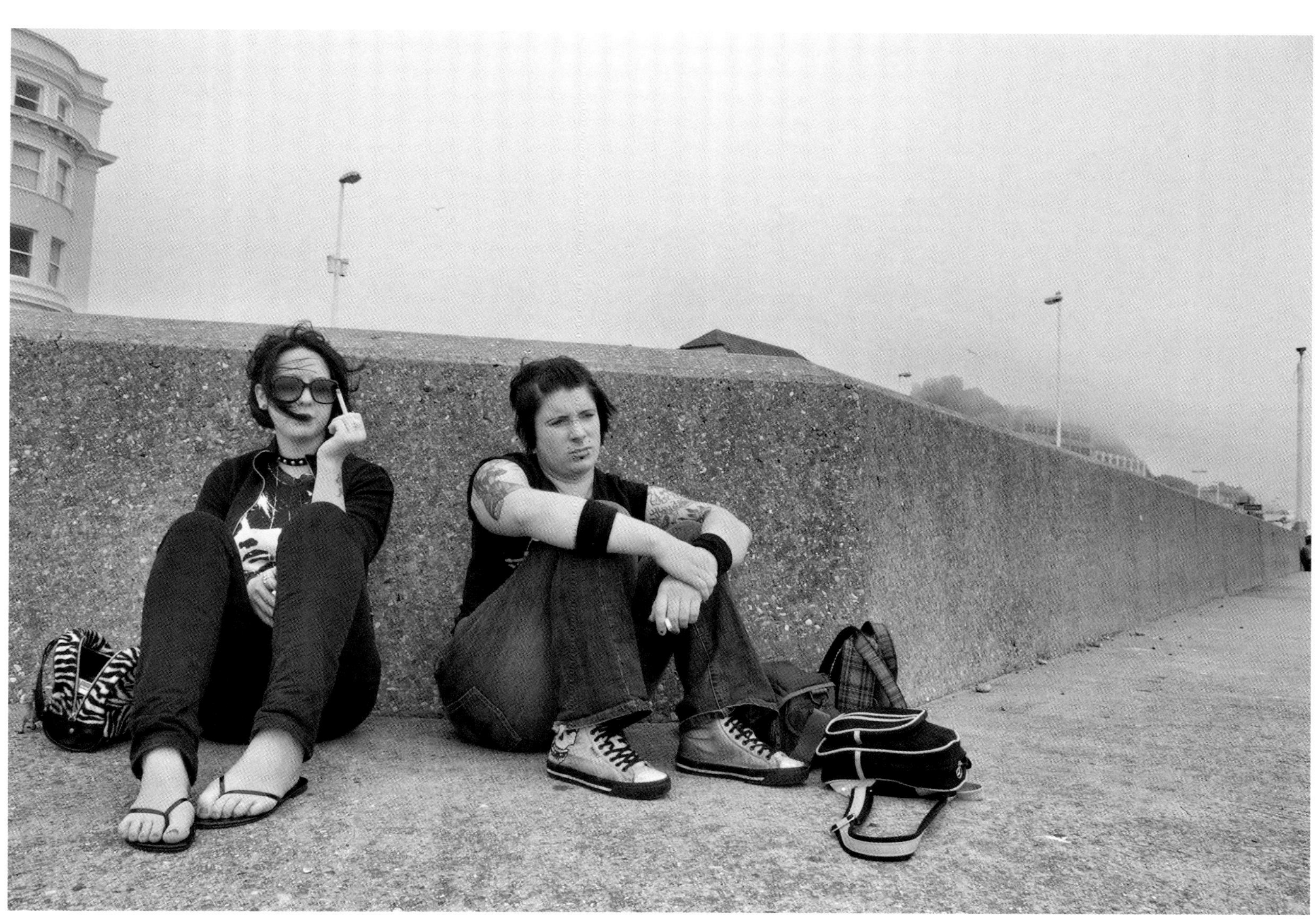

So not quite Sussex, but Kent.
The Isle of Sheppey to be exact.
South coast at least.

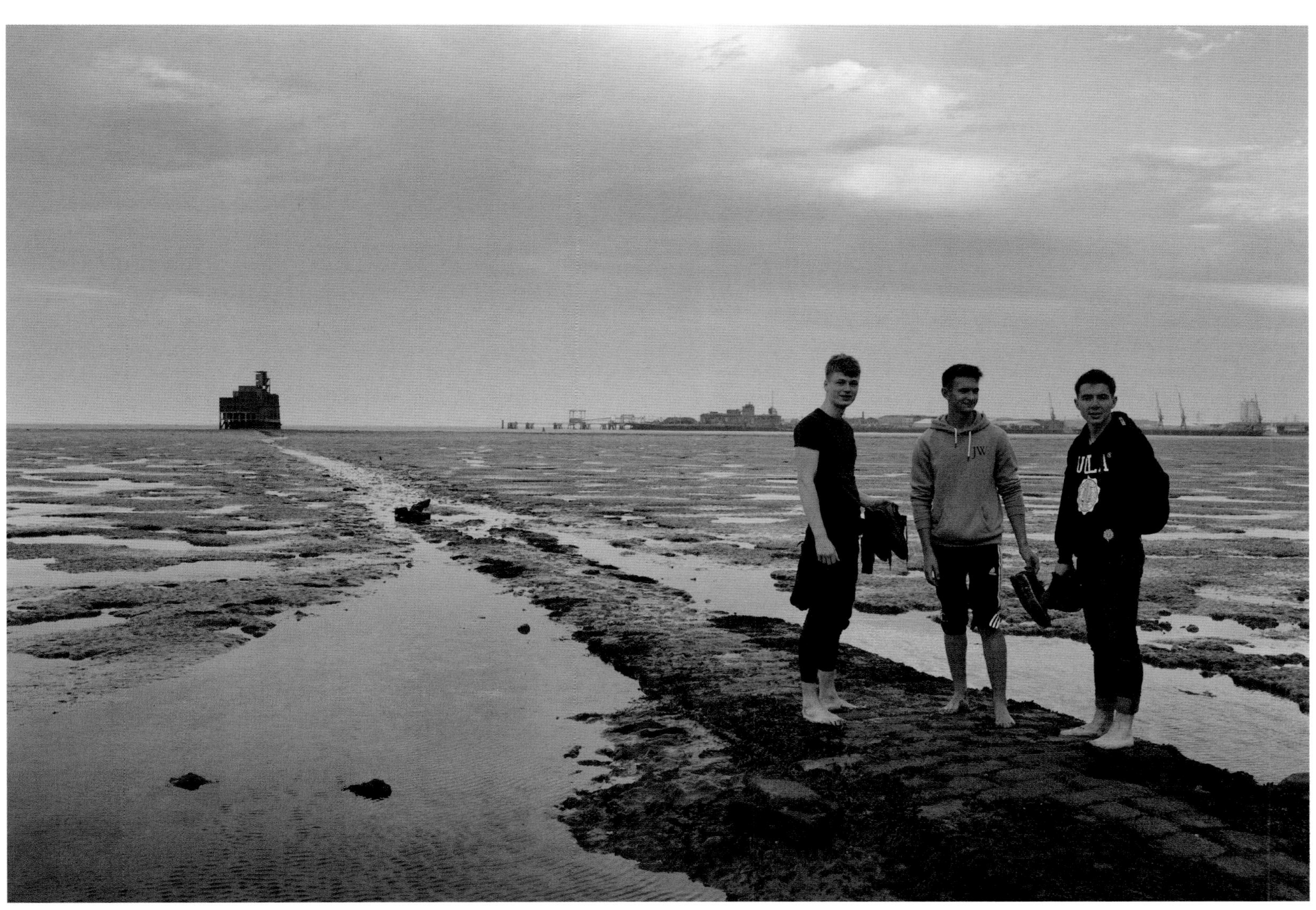

It could only happen in St Leonards.

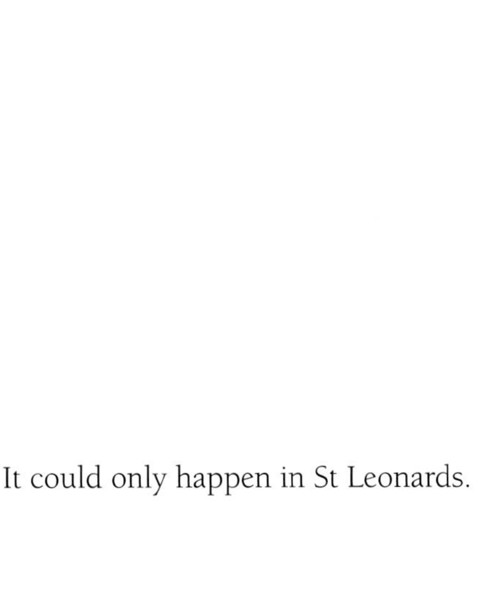

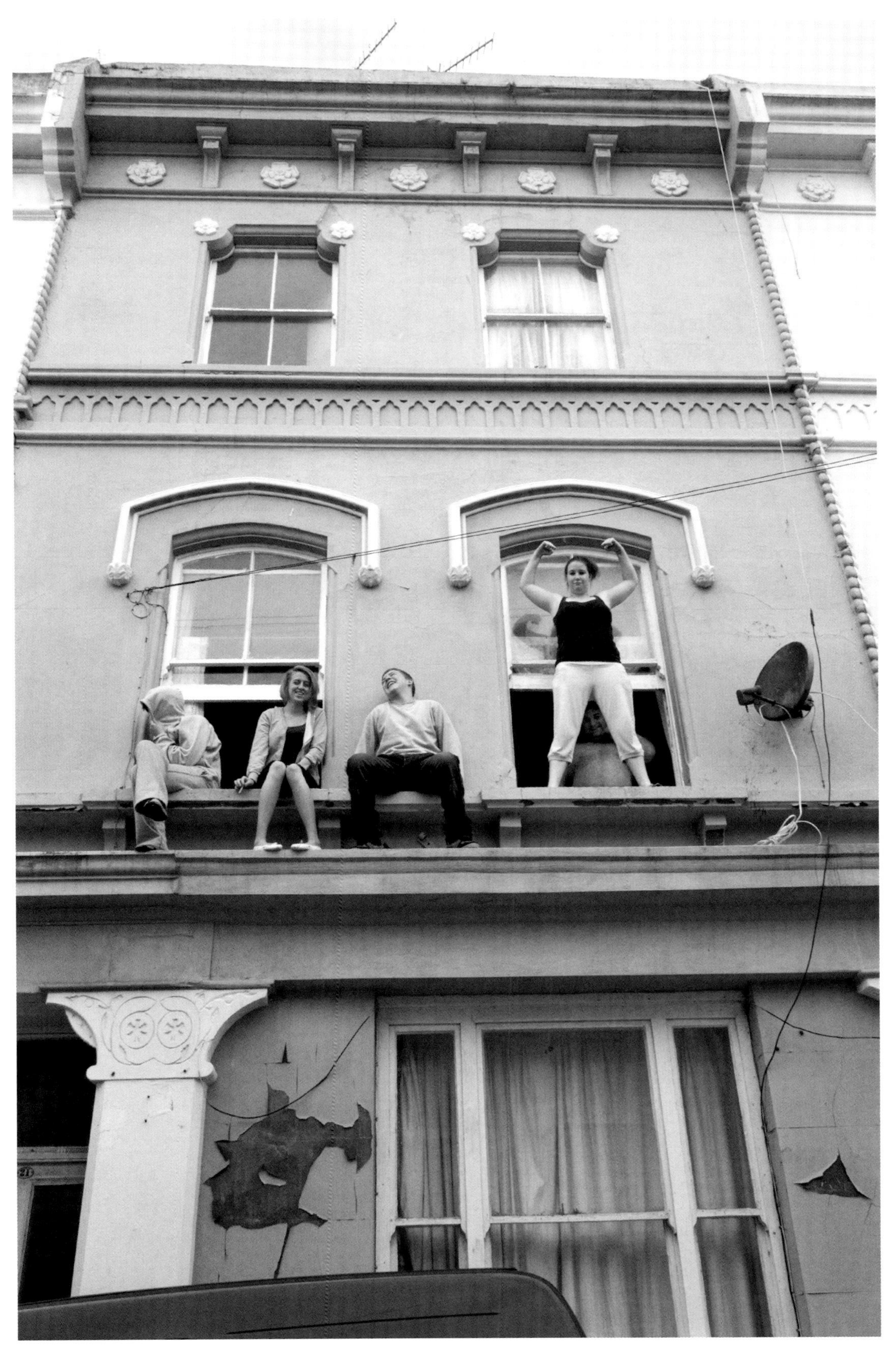

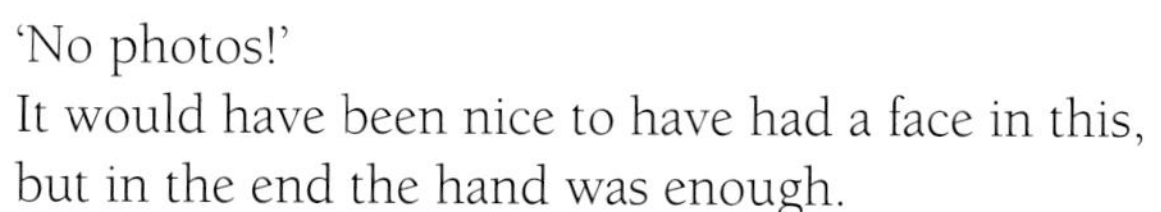

'No photos!'
It would have been nice to have had a face in this,
but in the end the hand was enough.

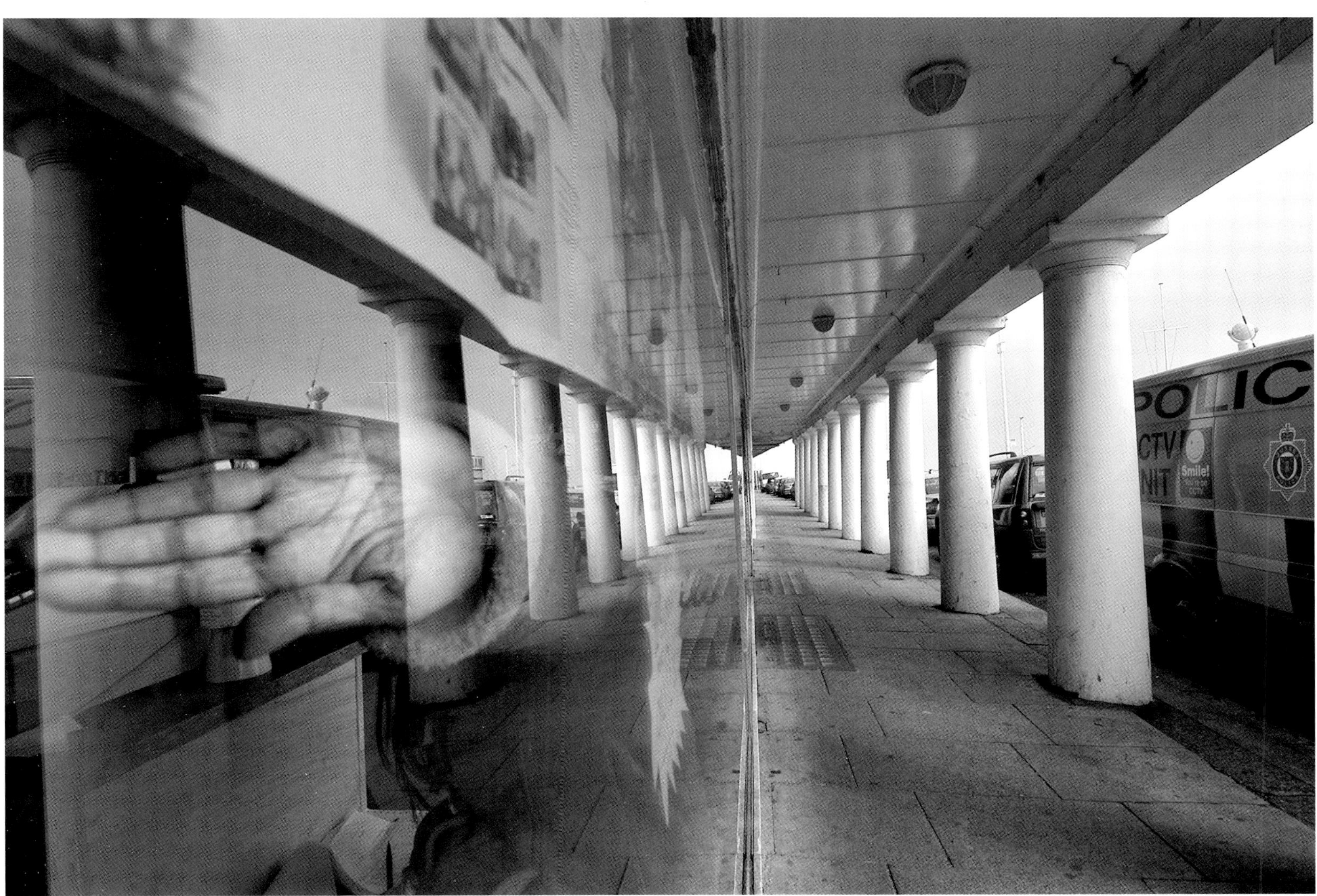
POLIC
CTV
NIT
Smile!
CTV

I often stop here and I often take photos from
this vantage point. This was not easy to frame up
and I had to stretch to get the kiddie in.

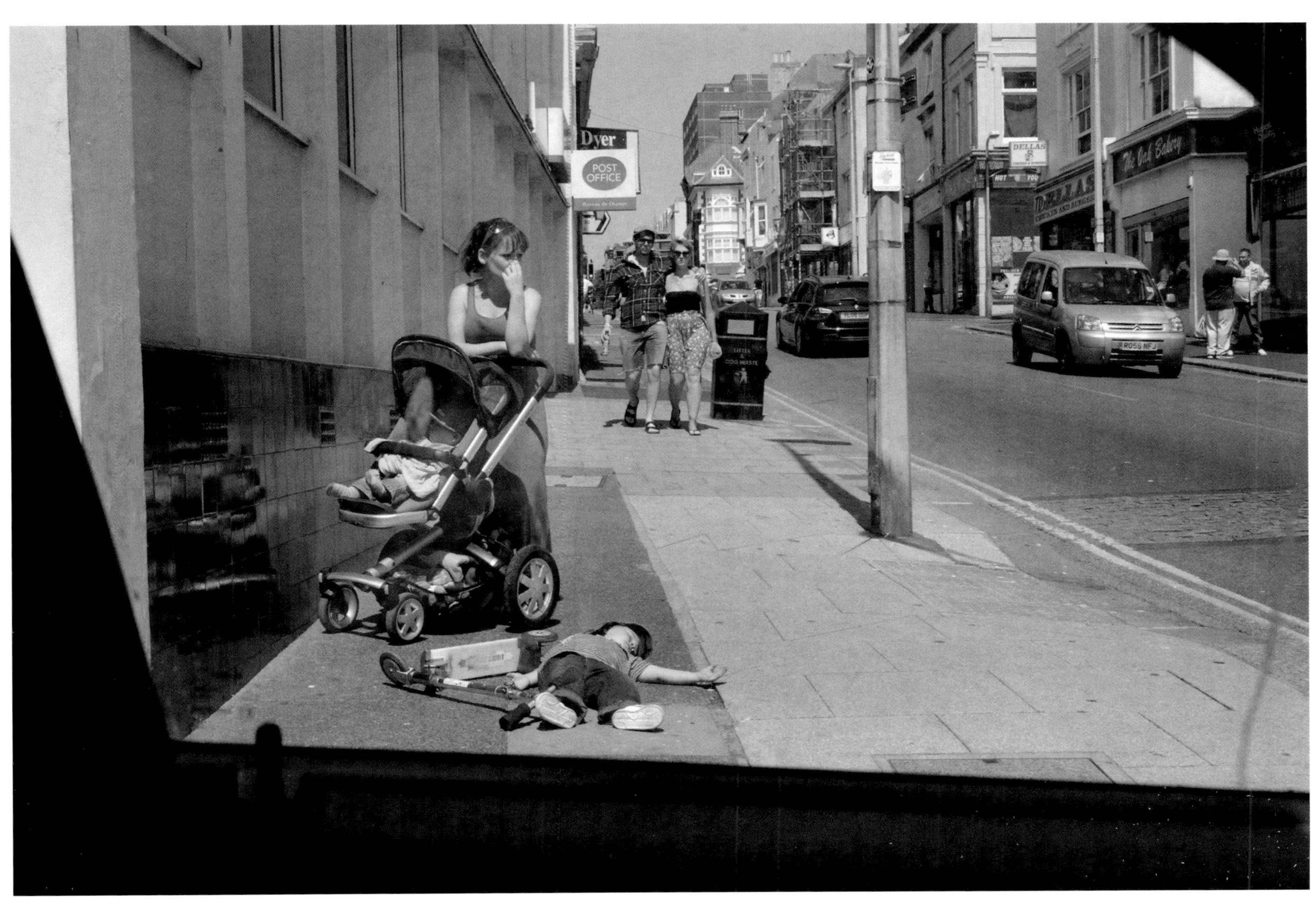

A junk store, a market place – near to
Debenhams, now defunct.

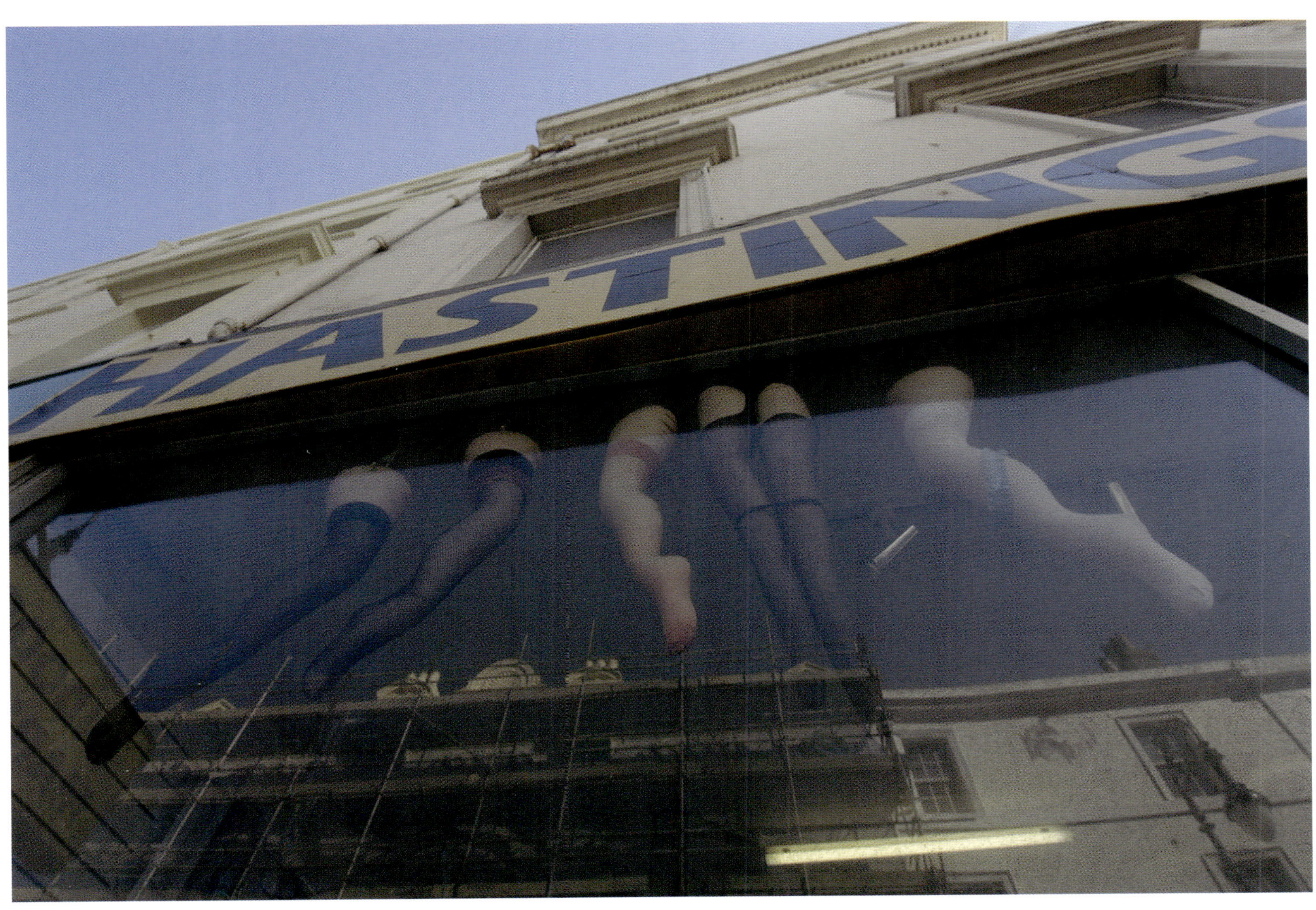

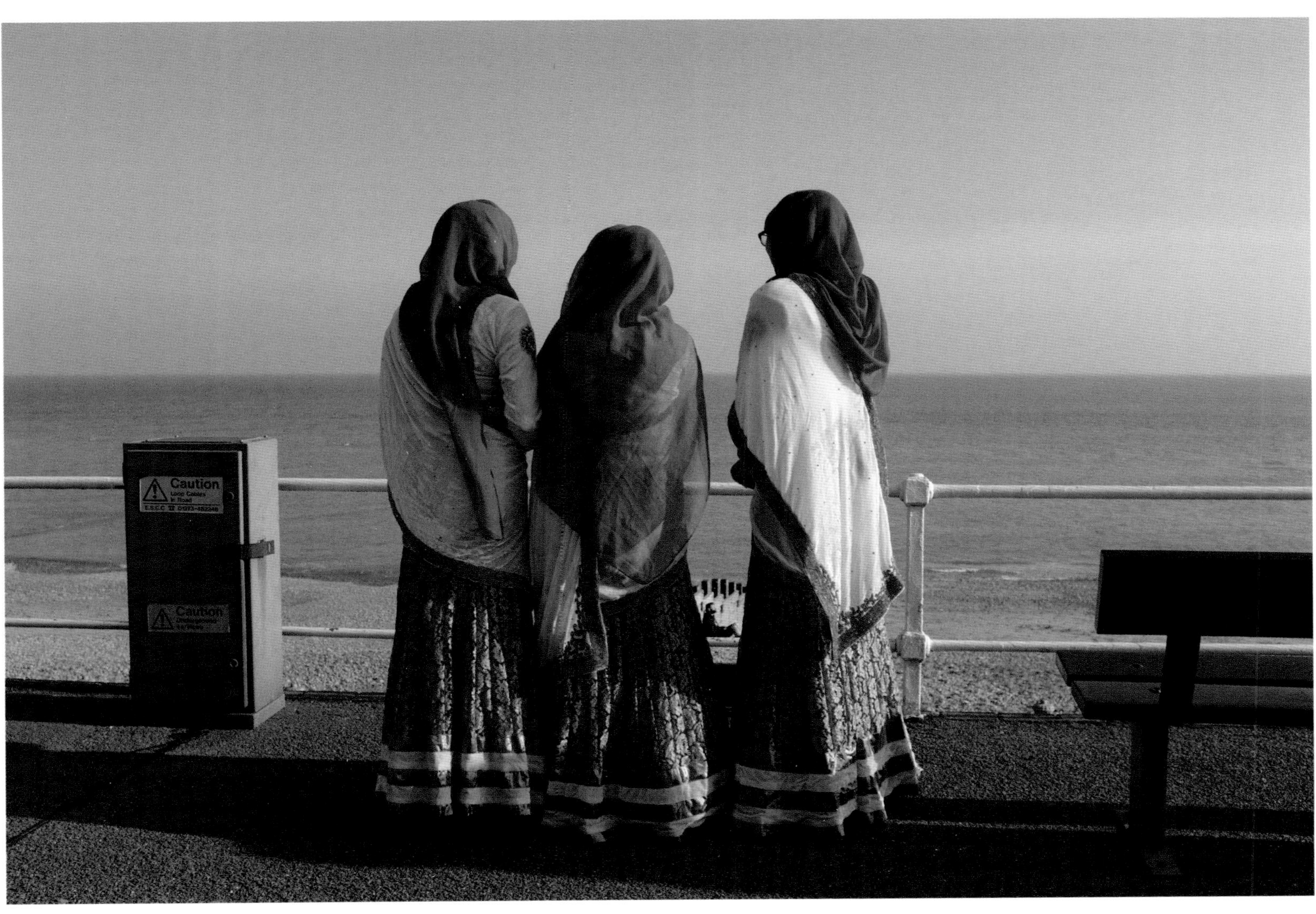

Not the sort of person you expect to be
sitting on a wall. With an old kettle in a bag.

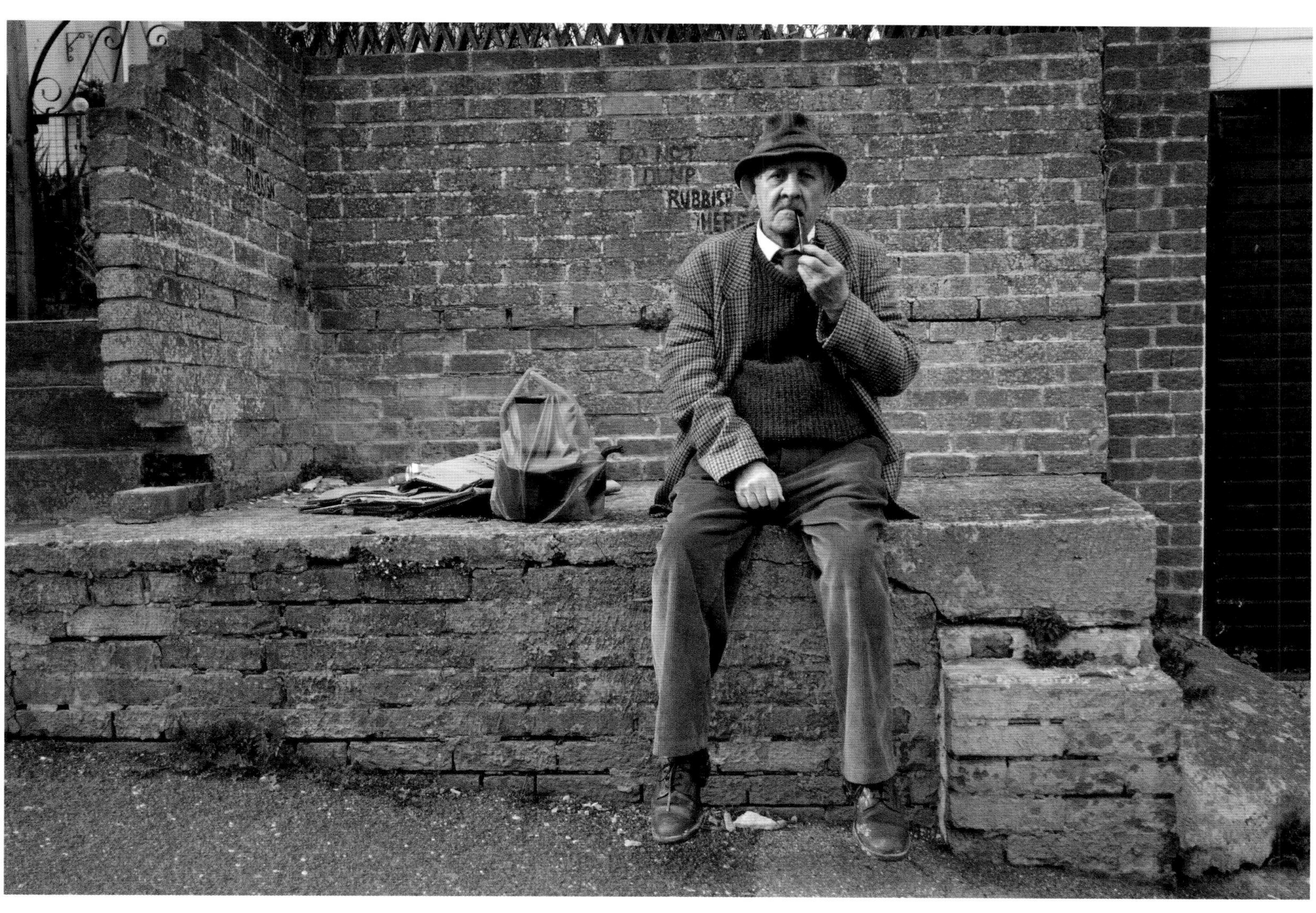
DO NOT
DUMP
RUBBISH
HERE

This was one of those moments when I was slightly
torn – 'Maybe I should help? I'll take a photograph
first, then help'. I could see they were blind drunk. I
did ask if they were ok afterwards.

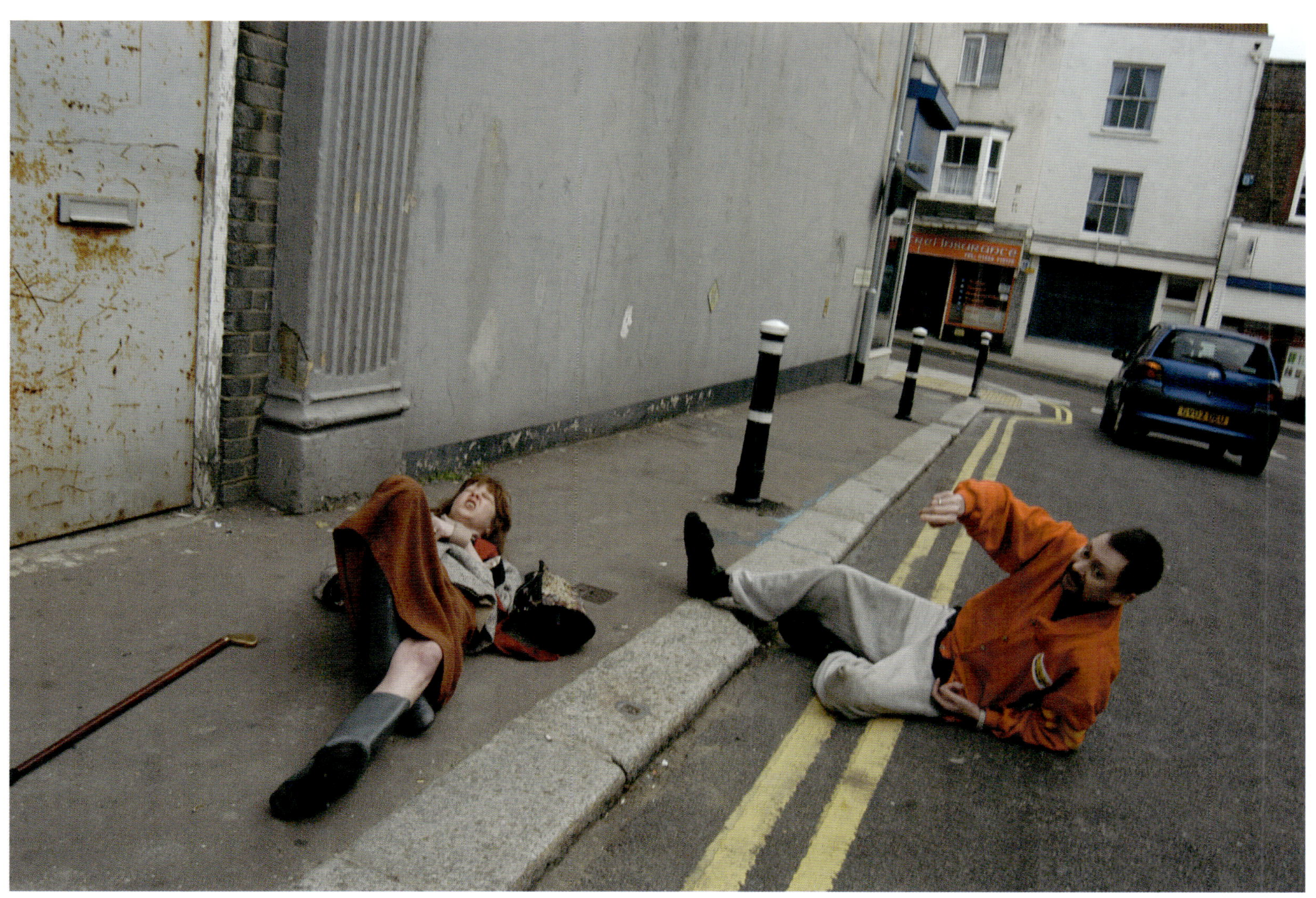

How much stuff this man had. First of all, it
shouldn't happen in this country – or any country
– that people have to live like that. Secondly, the
mystery of the quantity of the bags. That was the
thing that got me. There are a lot of street sleepers
along the front on the prom. The bags intrigued
me. So I decided to drive down to see him. I got
out of the car. I tried a walk-by picture of him, but
that didn't feel right – doing it with subterfuge. I
asked him if he minded me photographing the bags.
He didn't mind. I backed up further, and included
him. Then I went through the guilt again. What am
I doing? Am I taking advantage to make art out of
him? All photographers go through the same thing.
Sometimes you just cannot approach someone.
Other times you go and ask them.
I went back a few days later to see if he needed
anything. He was there. He asked for a cup of coffee
and a hot chocolate. I got him both – the café owners
also gave me some sweets to pass on. He seemed
very grateful. I was glad I did that. Sometime later,
he – and the bags – were gone.

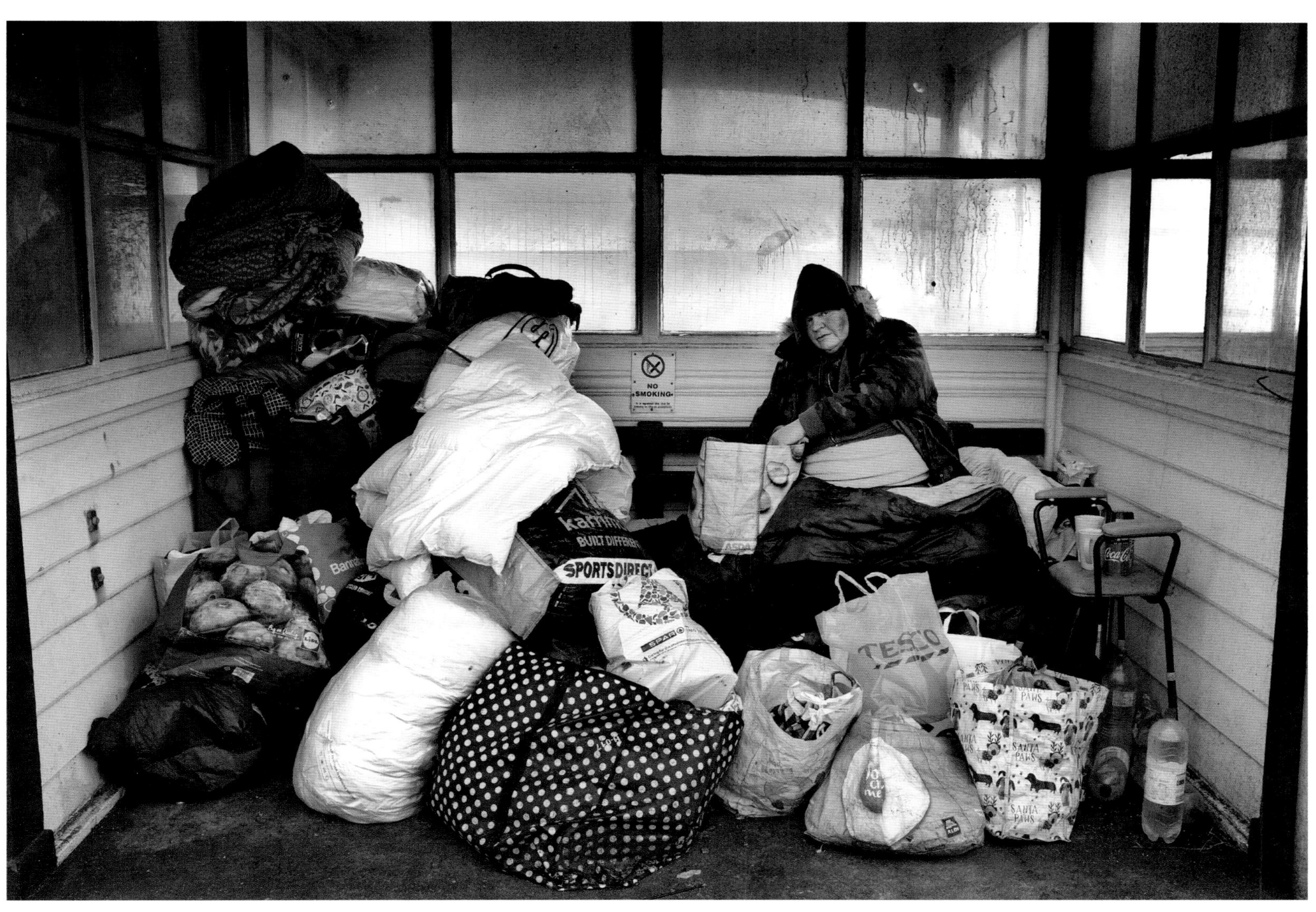

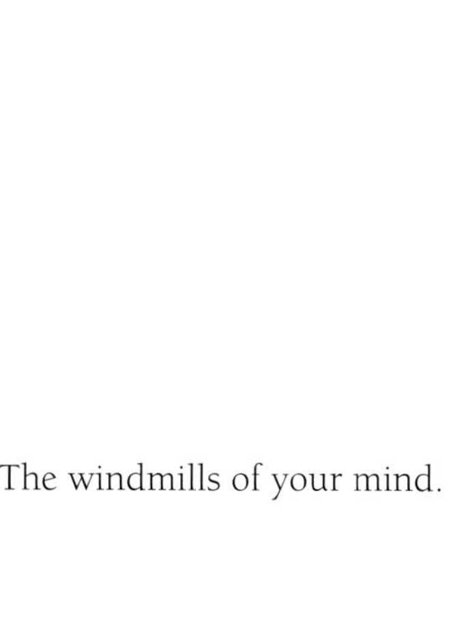

The windmills of your mind.

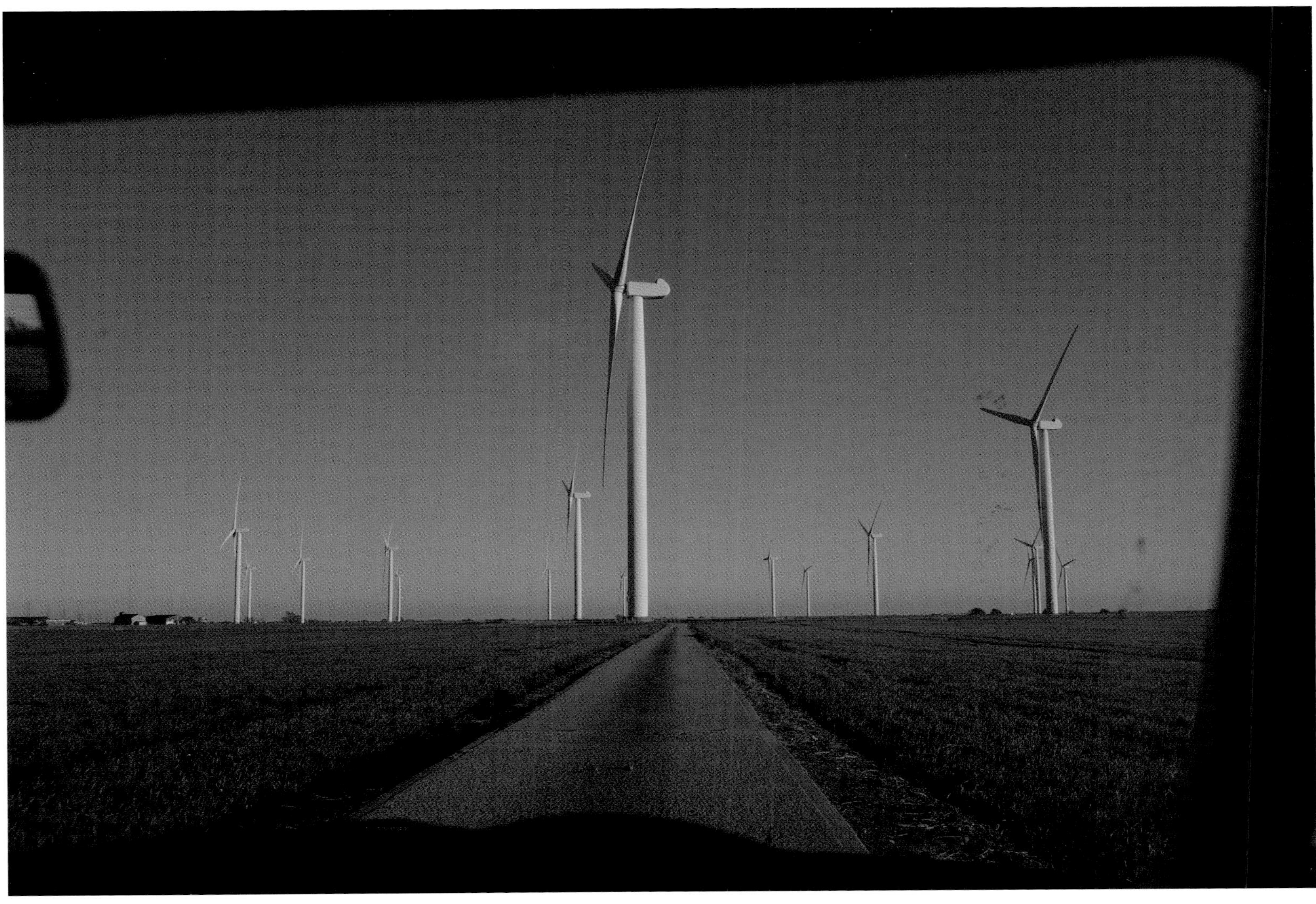

Me becoming the building. I made myself into the
thing I was photographing. Just for fun and to make
it weird. The church is locked – the big, iron key is
hanging on a wall in a building behind where I am
standing. Visitors are expected to return it to the hook.
And they do. It's an amazing thing in this day and age.

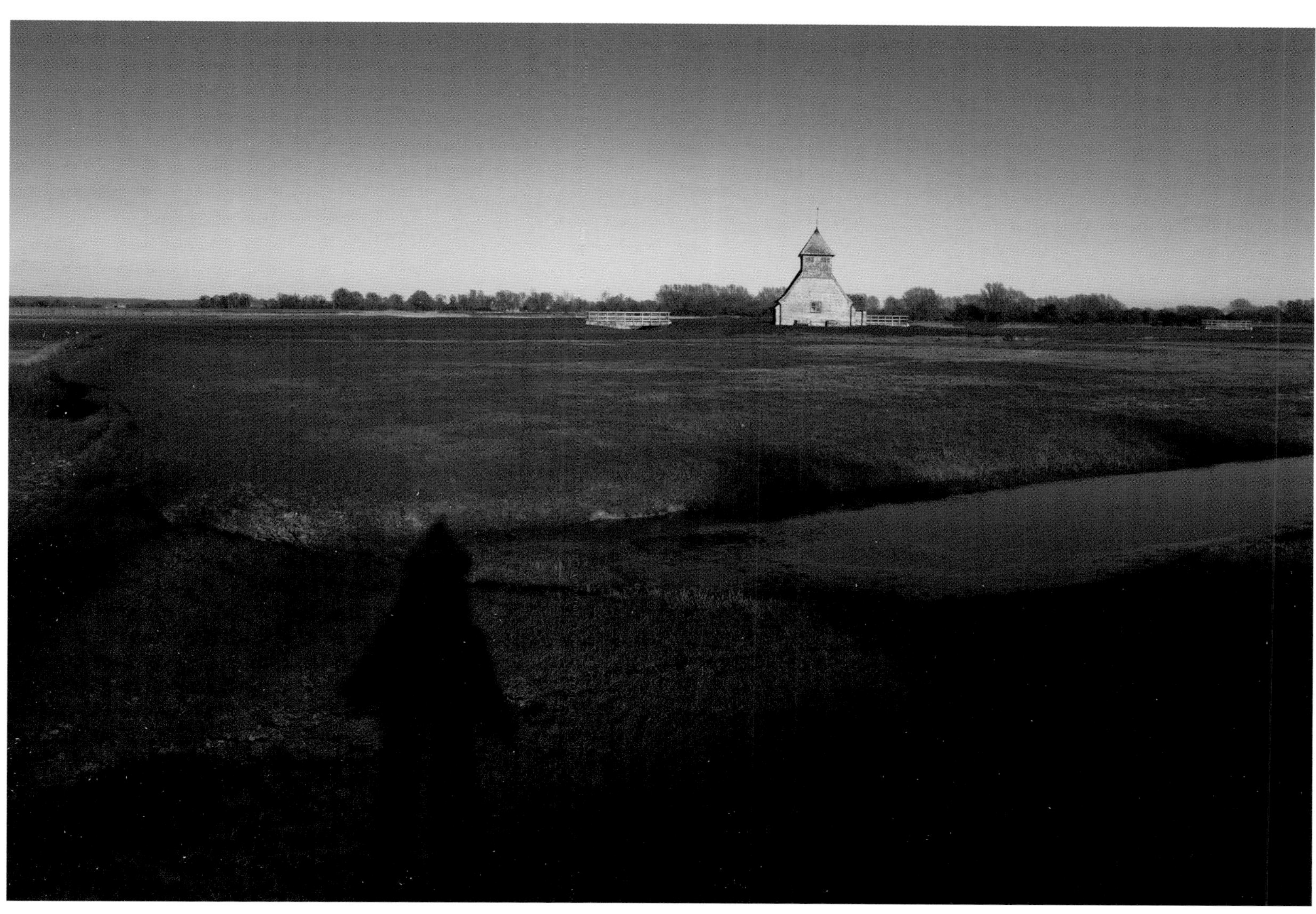

I like the idea of this picture. But when I look at it
I always wish I'd had the presence of mind to get
the cyclist's head into the shot. It really irritates me!
The pub transported to the promenade.
A touch of surrealism in a Hastings' pub.

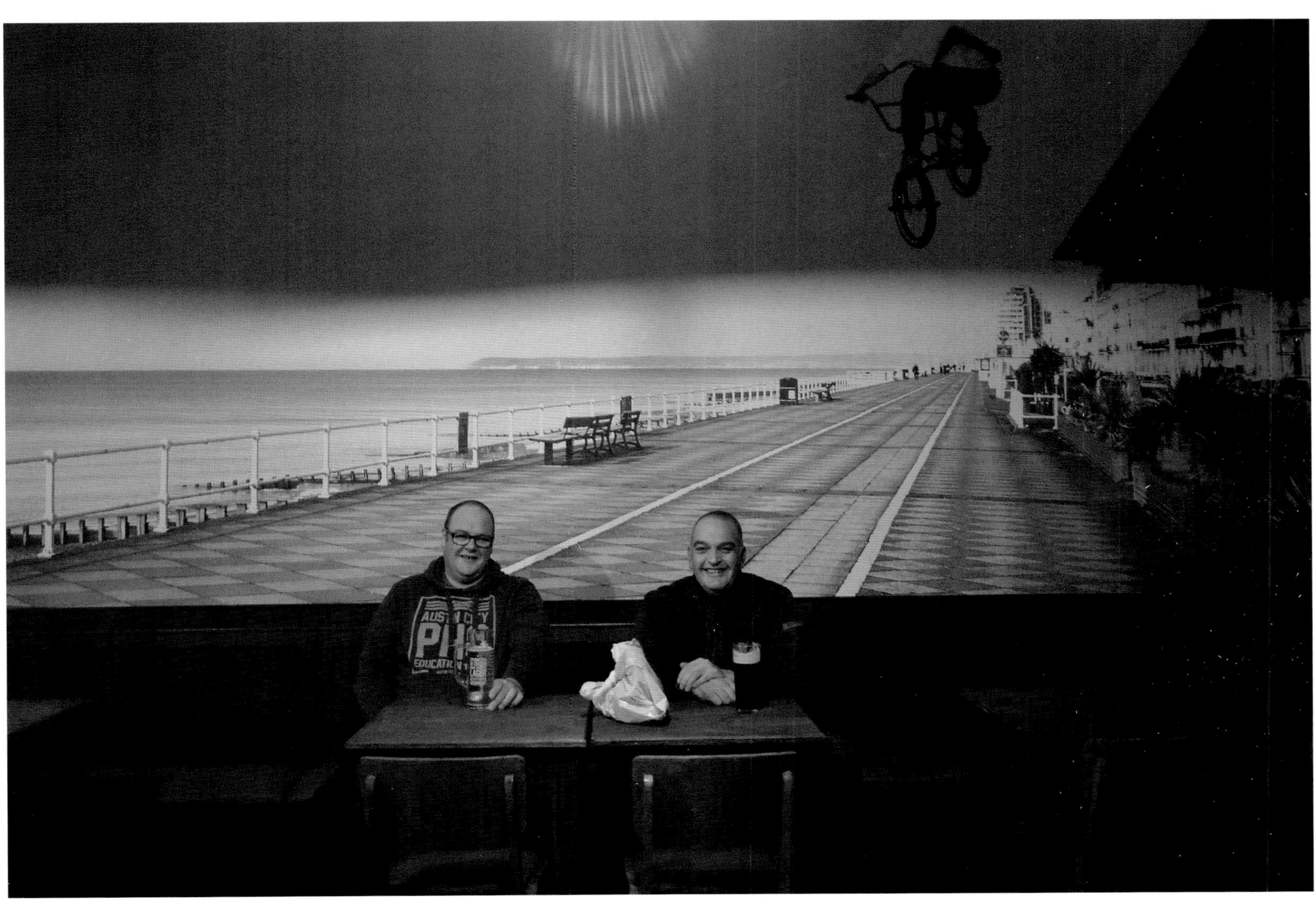

Margaret and her daughter. I've seen her around
Hastings for many years and I always wondered about
her. When I asked her if I could take her picture,
Margaret stood to attention for me. She obviously has a
military background.

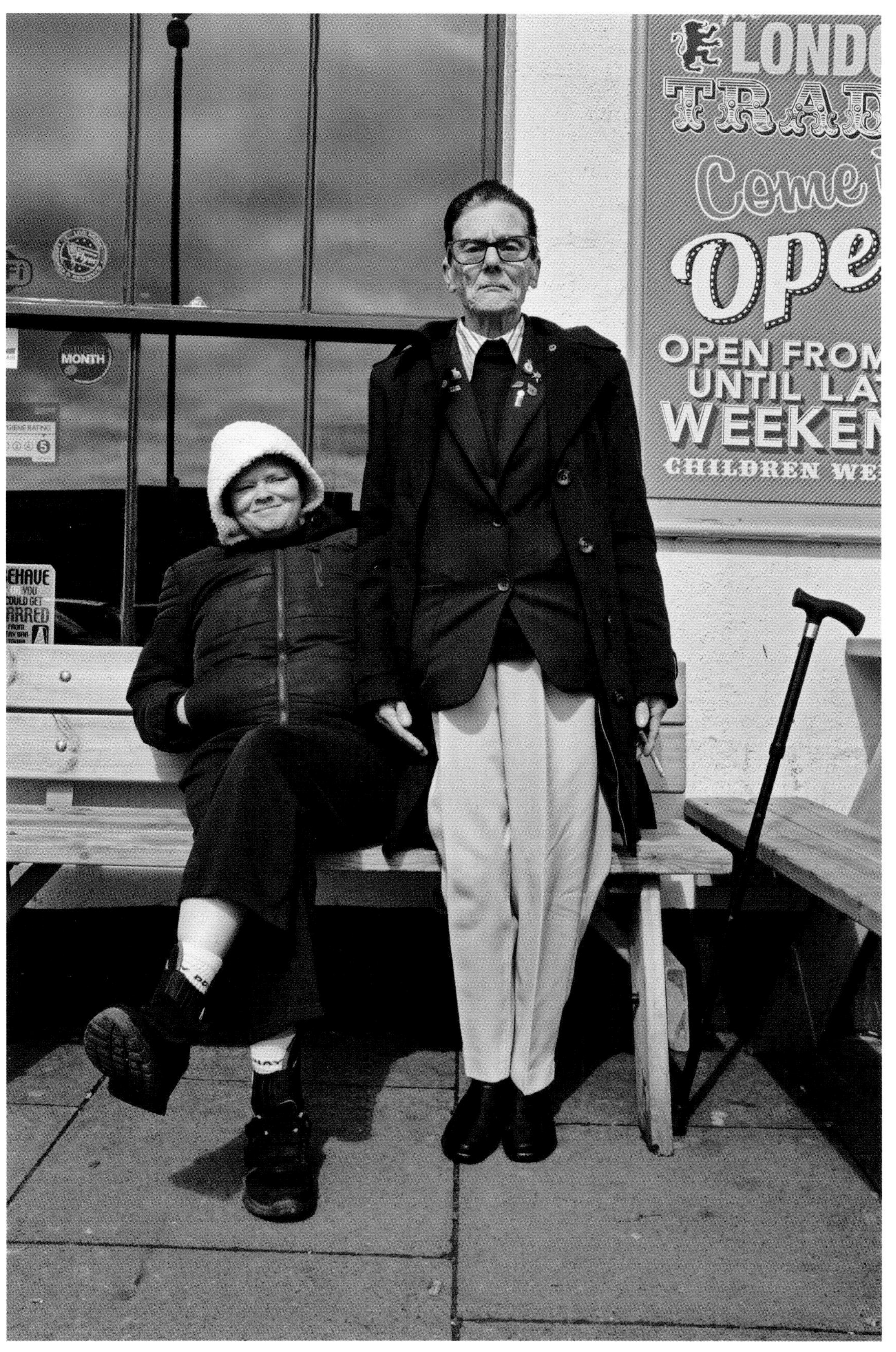
LONDO
TRAD
Come i
OPE
OPEN FROM
UNTIL LAT
WEEKEN
CHILDREN WE

Dear old Richard. I've been photographing him for thirty years, as he's aged. The first time I photographed him, he was sunlit in a place called Church in the Wood. I lost that photograph and I've been trying to recapture that picture ever since. I kept promising to get a photo to him and last Christmas I finally framed one and delivered it to where I knew he lived.

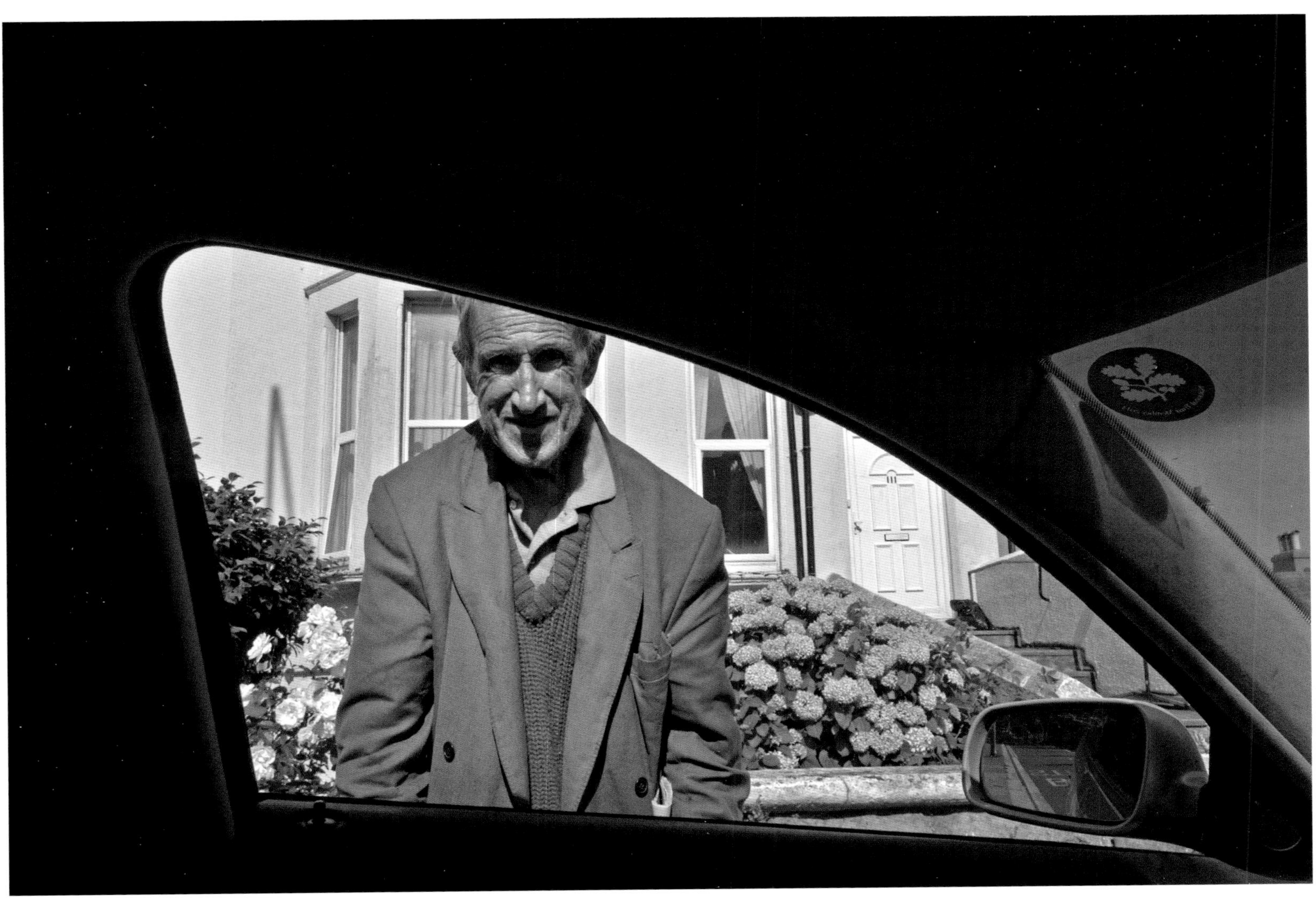

Down the years I've taken lots of pictures of messages
that come through the telly. I like the message but
I wasn't so sure about the background. But I feel
affection for the background – it is where I live.

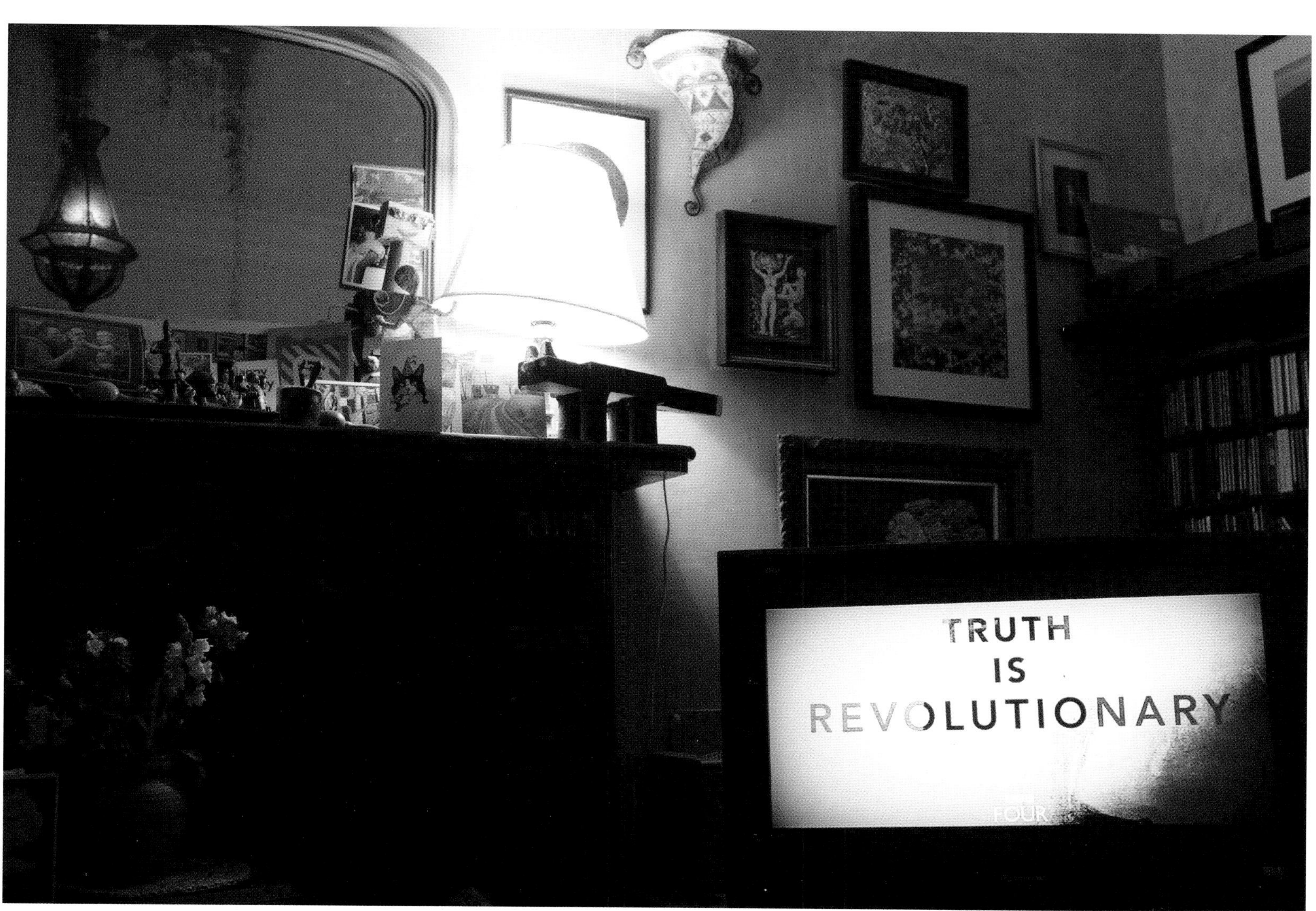
TRUTH
IS
REVOLUTIONARY
FOUR

The Lighthouse.
Jen and I – very early on in our relationship – had
gone up to Beachy Head. It was a beautiful blue day.
No sign of cloud. We got to the cliff edge and looked
over. We were amazed to see a low bank of cloud with
the lighthouse peeping out. It was perfect. I could
have jumped for joy.

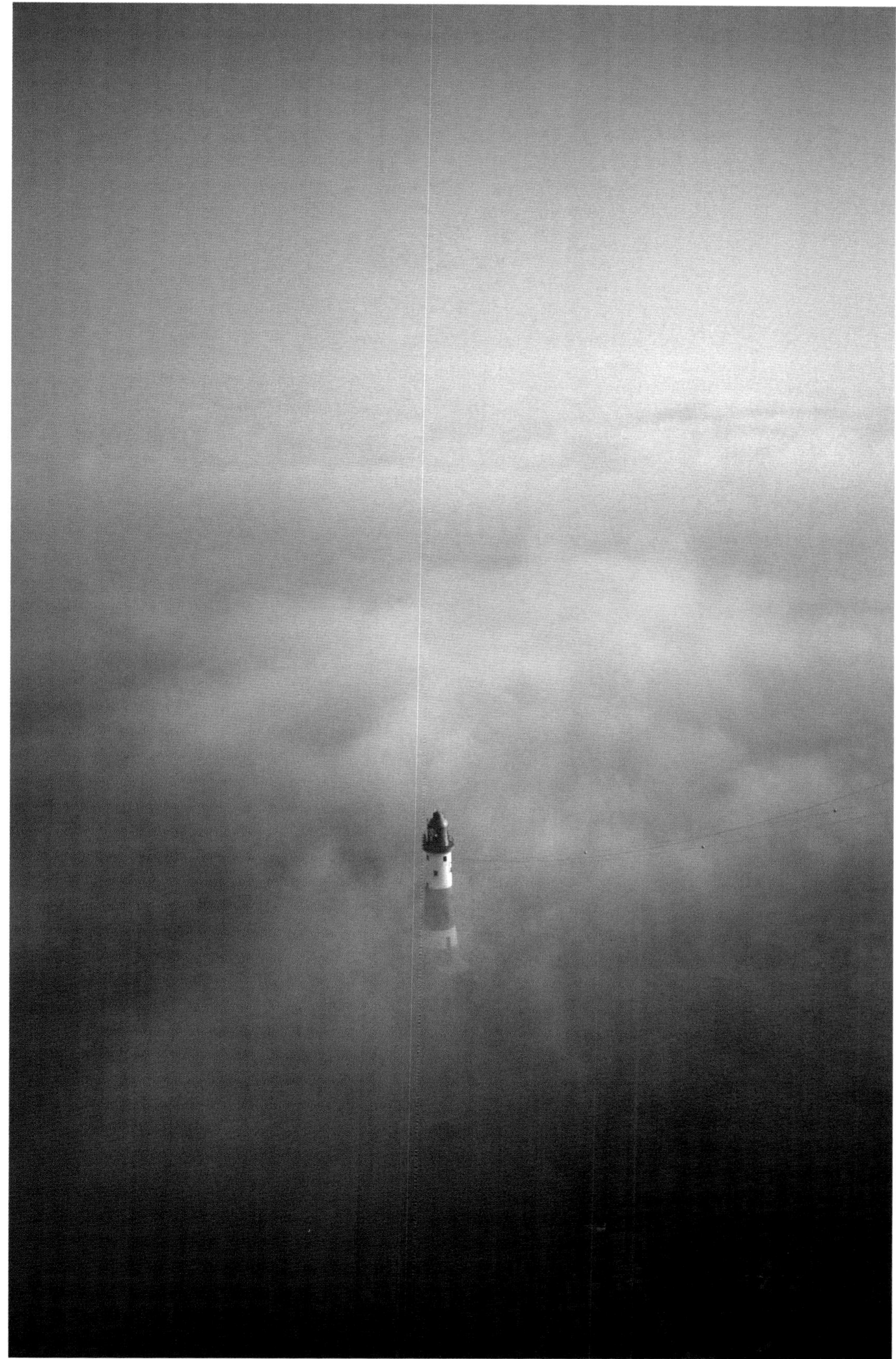

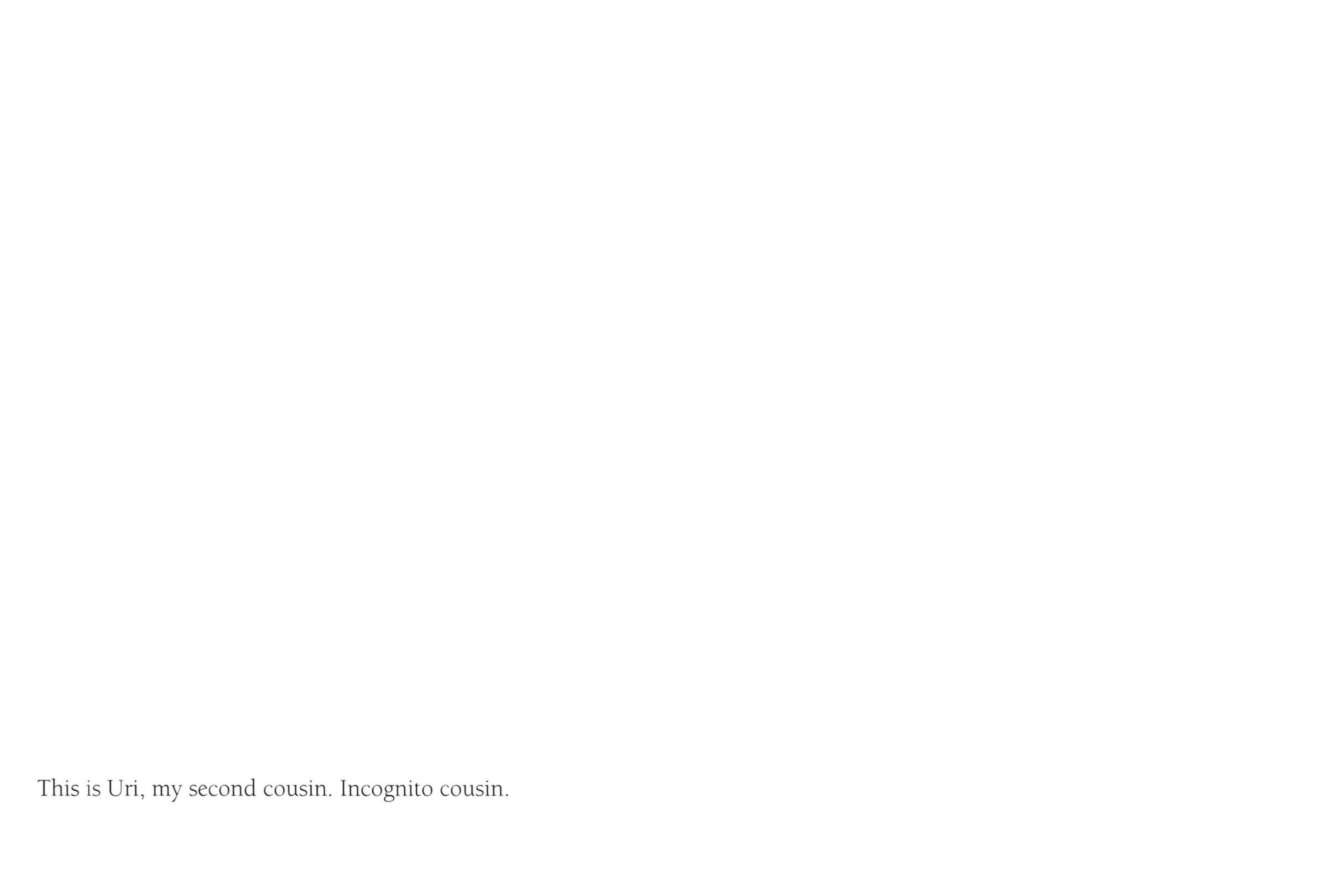

This is Uri, my second cousin. Incognito cousin.

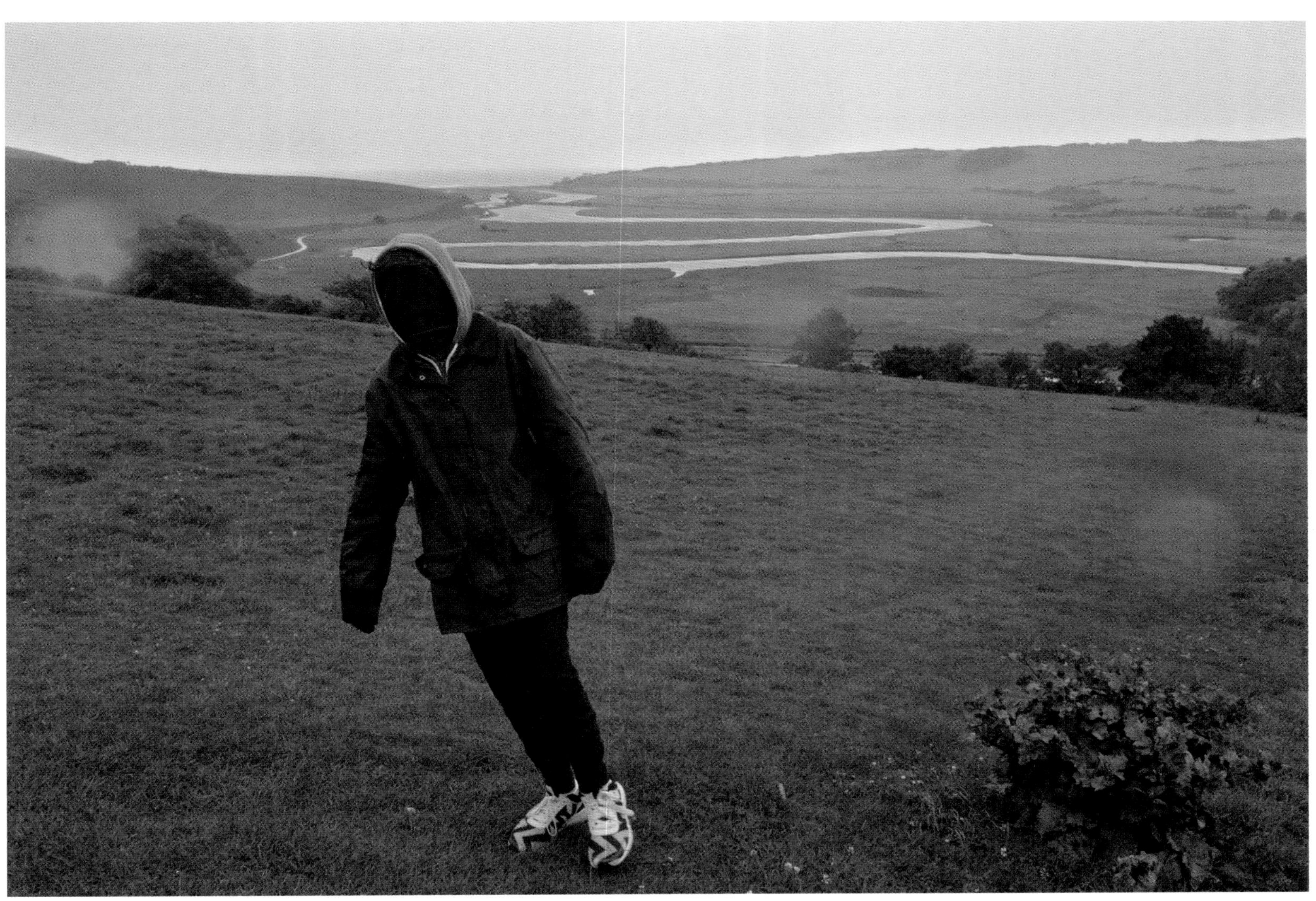

Pett Level.
What I like about this picture, as my daughter
pointed out to me, is its resemblance to one of those
chalk, trompe l'oeil paintings done on the pavement.
Like there is a floating field – now I can't look at it
without seeing that. And four separate flocks of birds
– all in one shot.

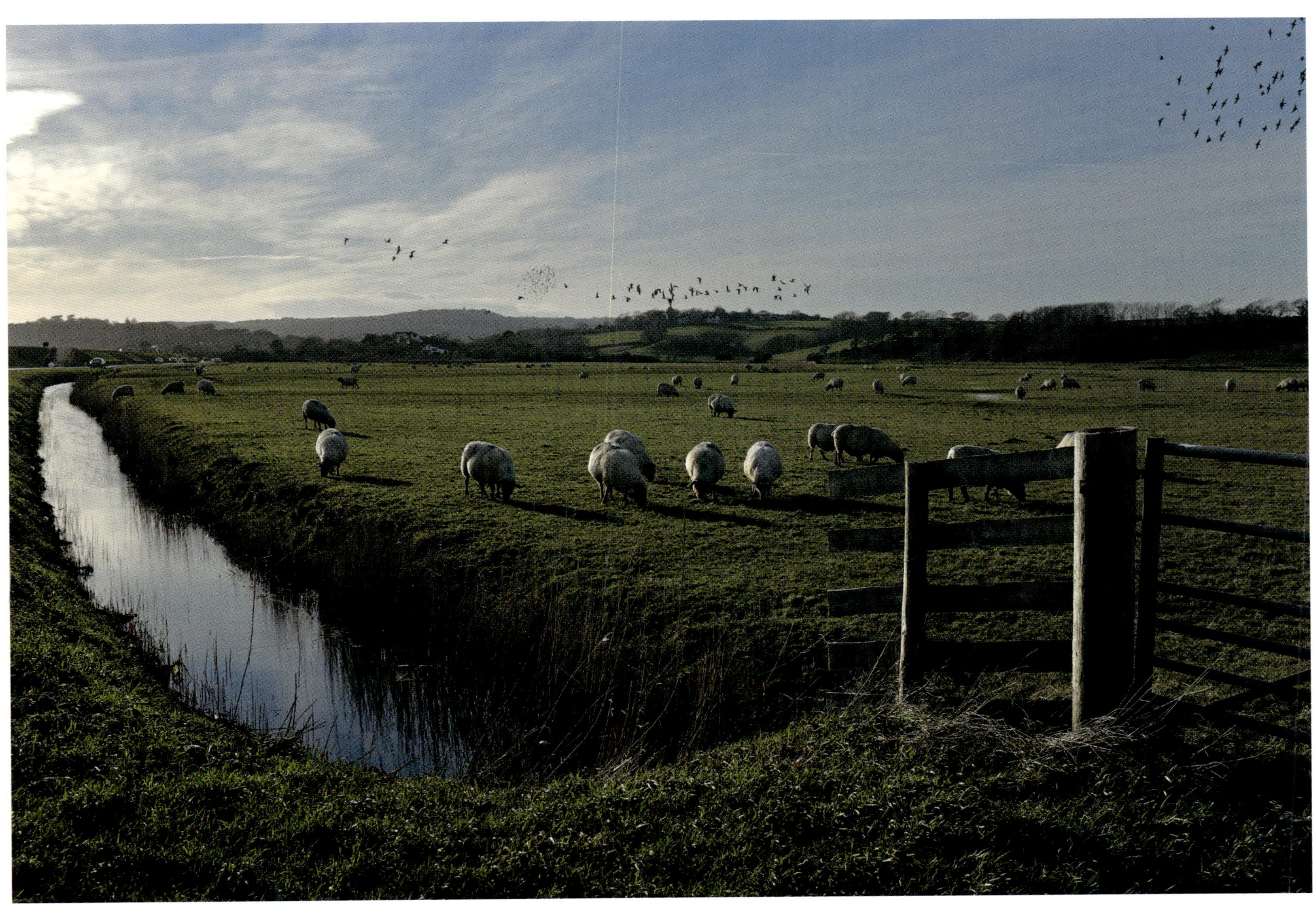

Hastings' old pier. Unbelievably, taken in
May one year! It could be Russia.

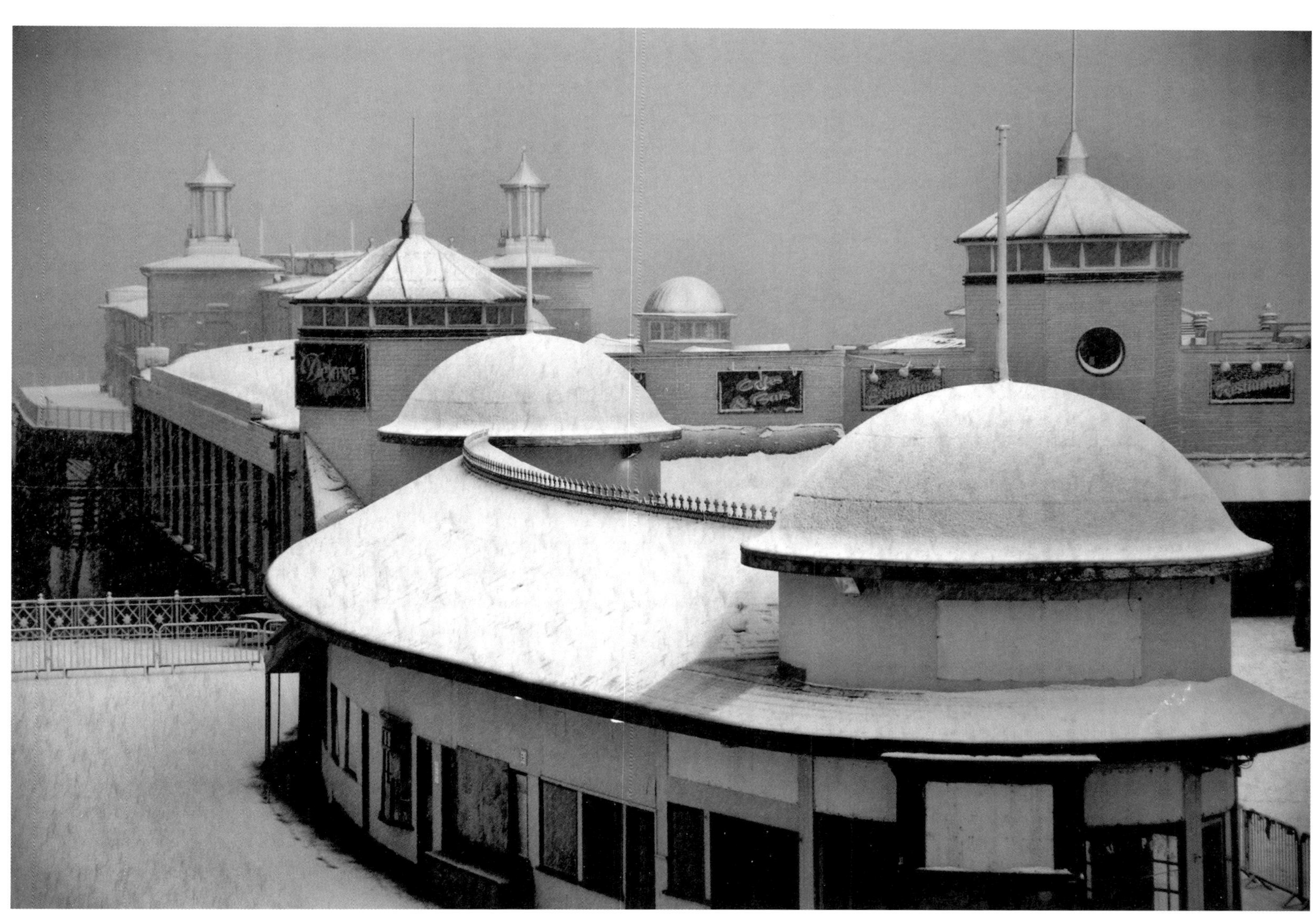

I know these people. I can't remember who they are
but I know them. I like the orange and blue going on,
all the bits and bobs.

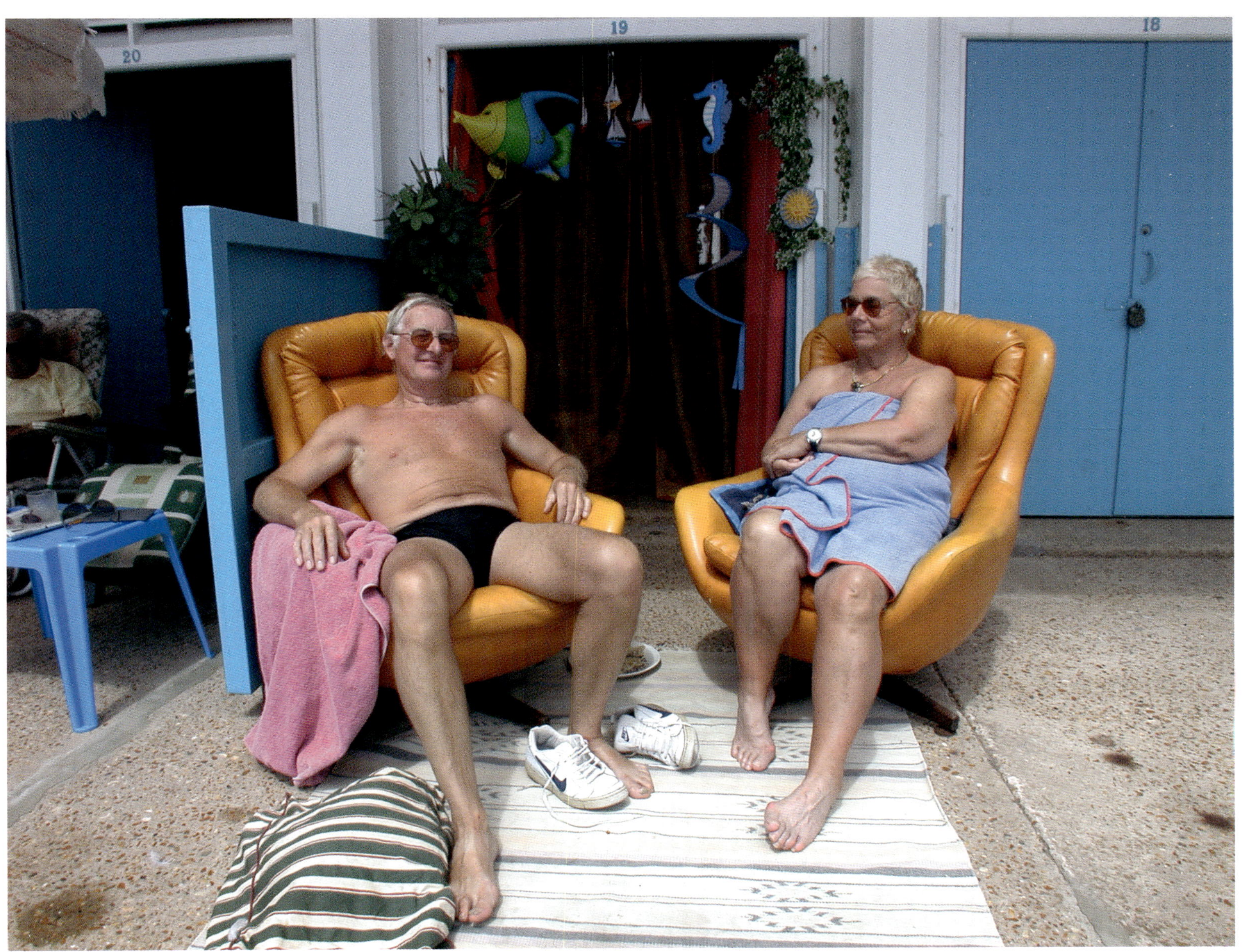

I was having this long conversation on the pavement
outside the takeway with two other people. And I
could see this kiddie pushing his hands and cheeks
against the window. But kiddie paranoia overtook me
to a degree. I didn't want to get accosted by mum.
Eventually I got brave enough to make it known to
his mum that I wanted to take a photo. And then she
showed me who she was talking to on her phone. And
I thought, 'that's it – permission.' I presumed there
were three generations in this picture – the little one,
his mum and then her mum on the phone.

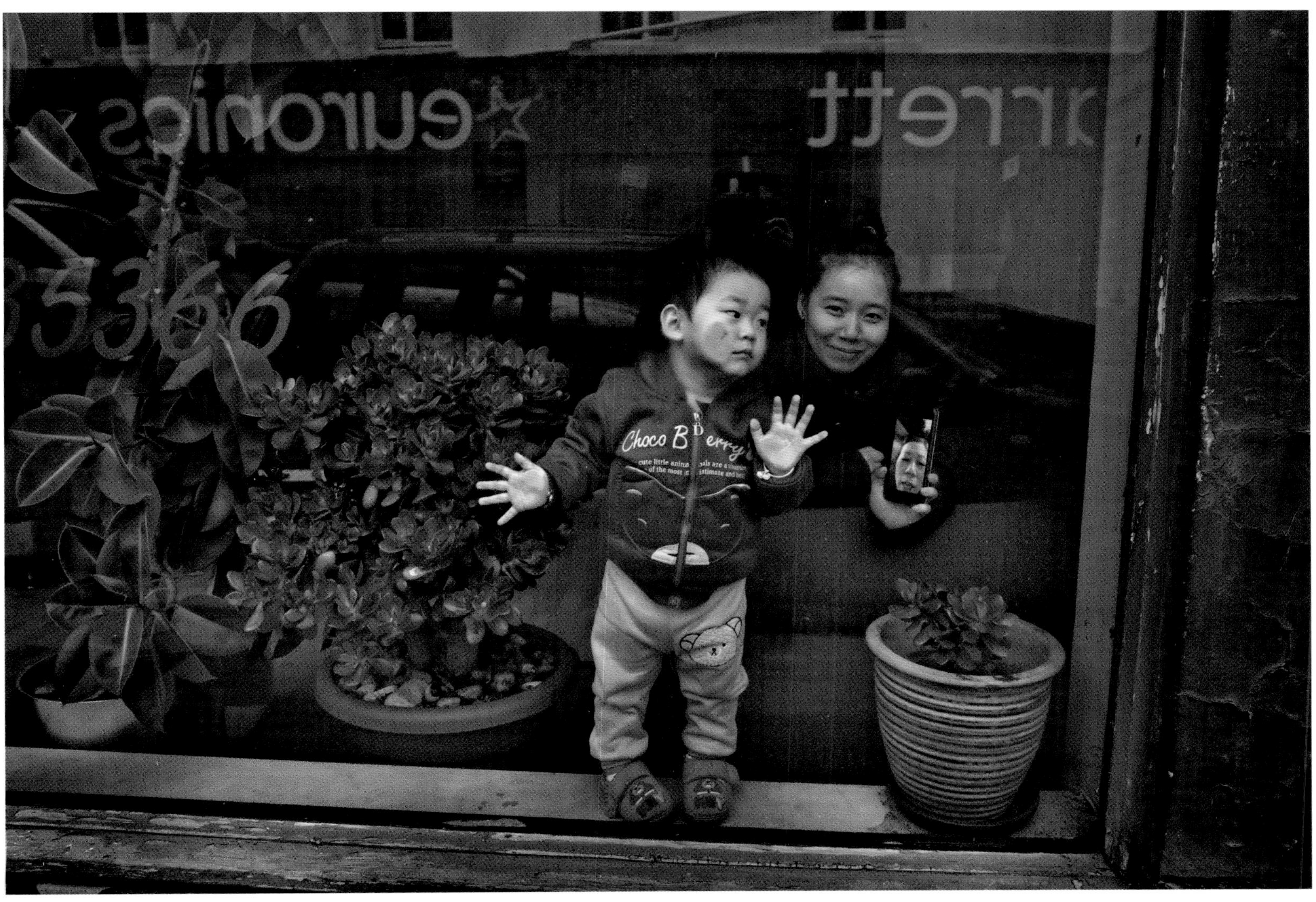

The Elvis Acrobats. A festival in St Leonards some
years ago. Not only was Elvis not dead, there were two
of them and they were acrobats. I like the composition.
Classically black and white.

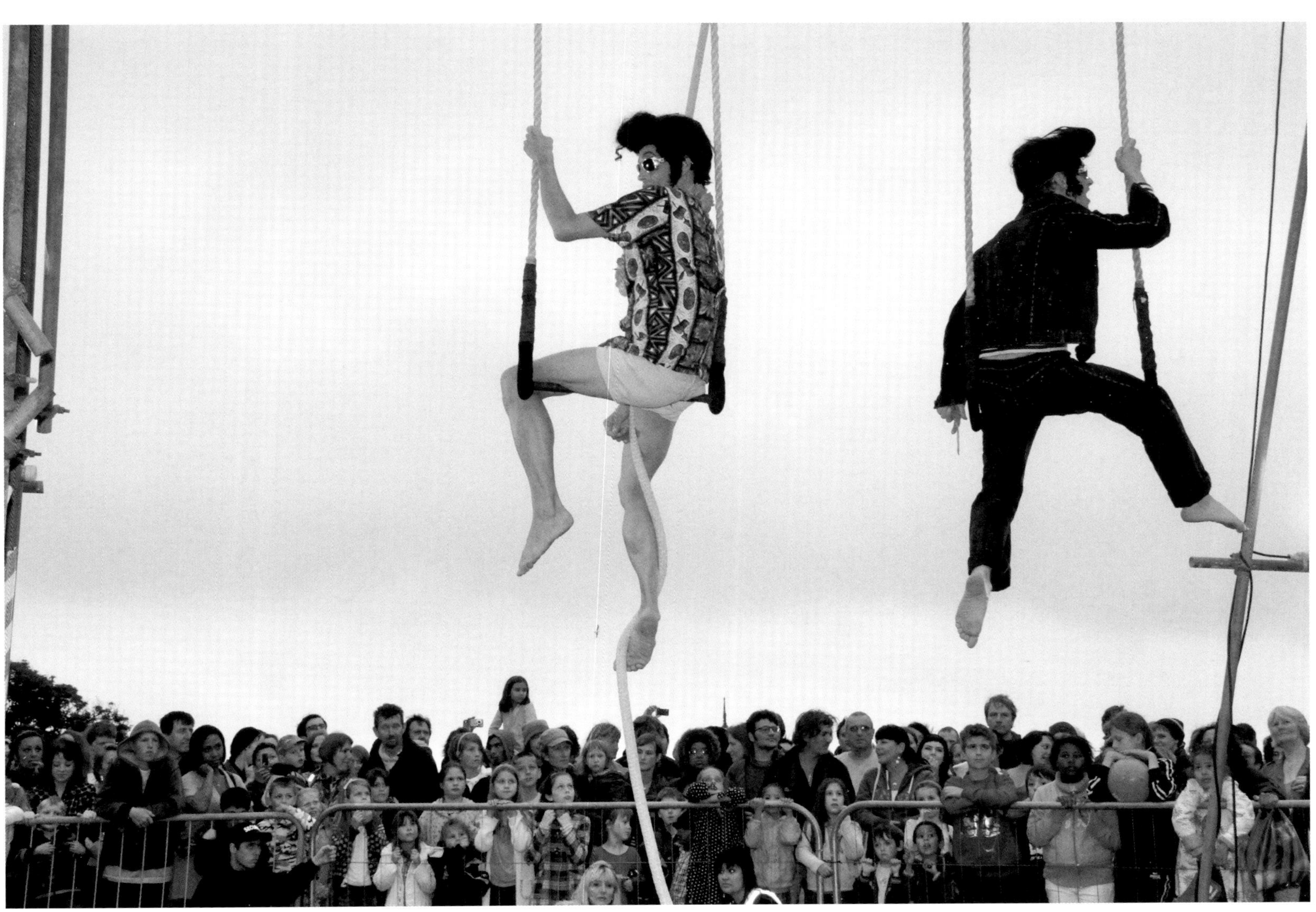

Meeting my neighbour, Tony the Hat, for the first
time. We both have an affinity for hats.

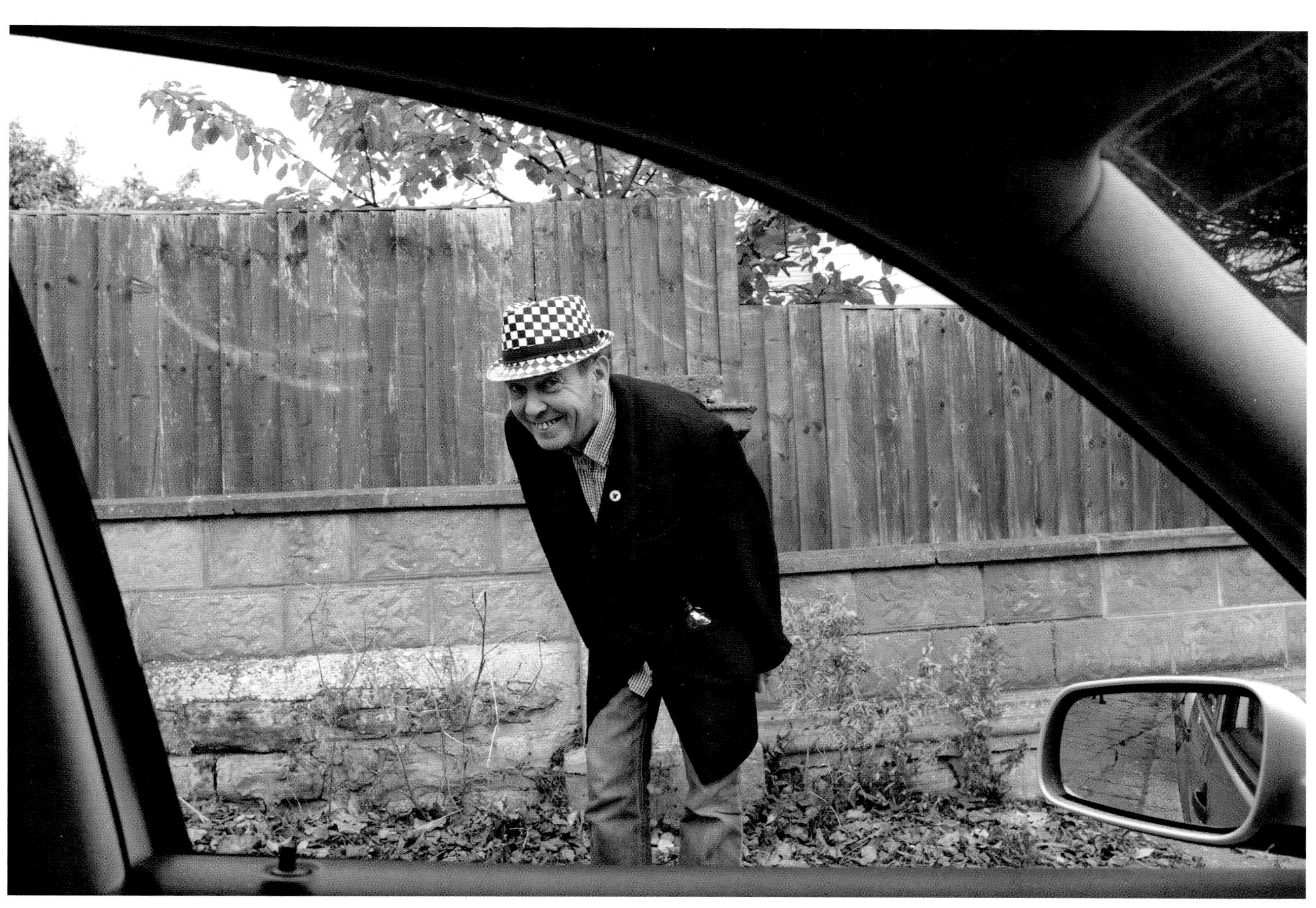

I made this into my Christmas card one year because
I thought it was so jolly. Not. All the elements – the
unstocked shelves, the 'smile you're on camera' sticker.
This was taken in the days before the gentrification of
St Leonards when we had empty shops on the high
street. Now they are all bistros.

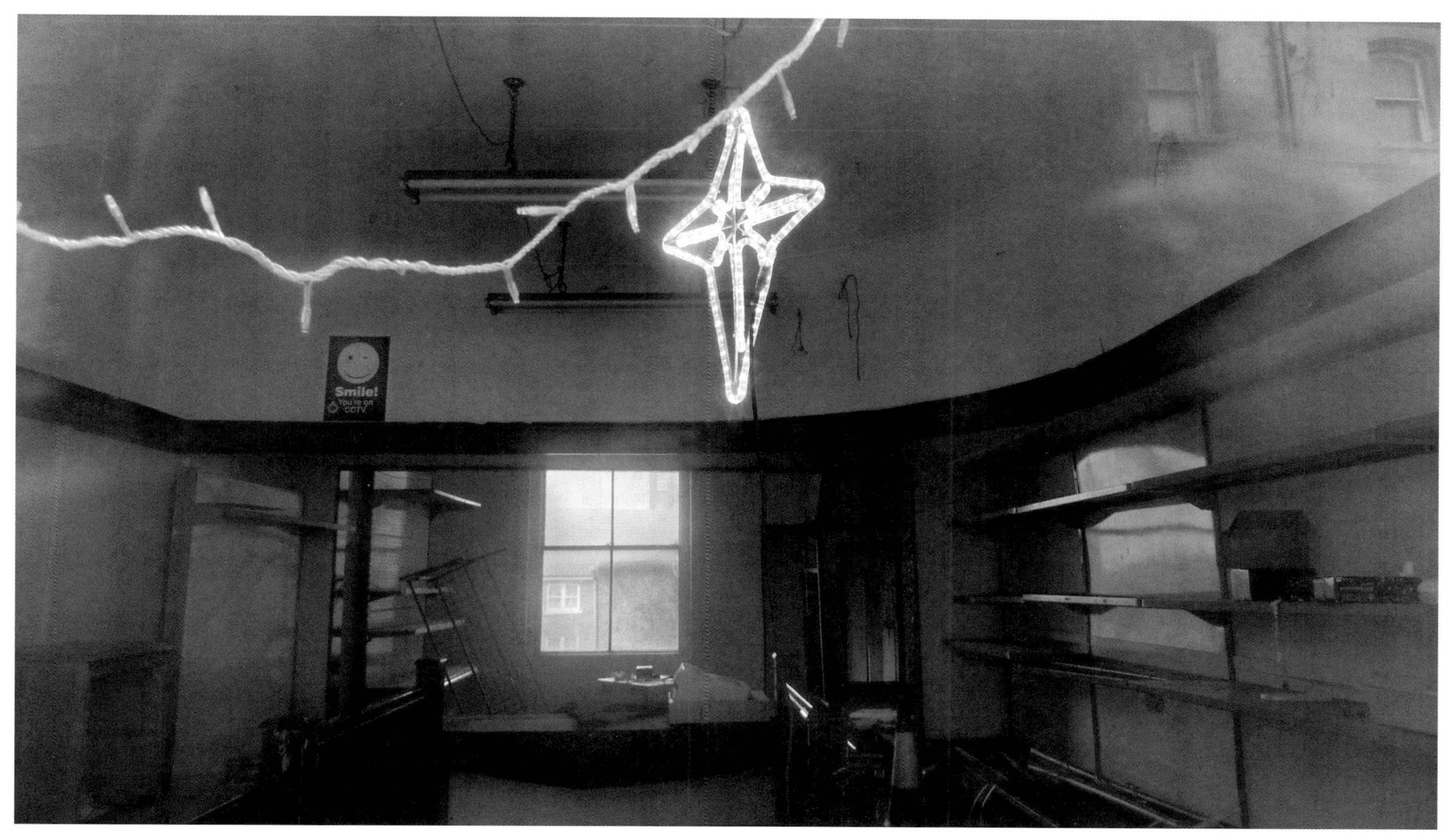

I was driving home at night down a road I'd driven a
thousand times before. It was particularly lovely that
day and the colours matched my dashboard.

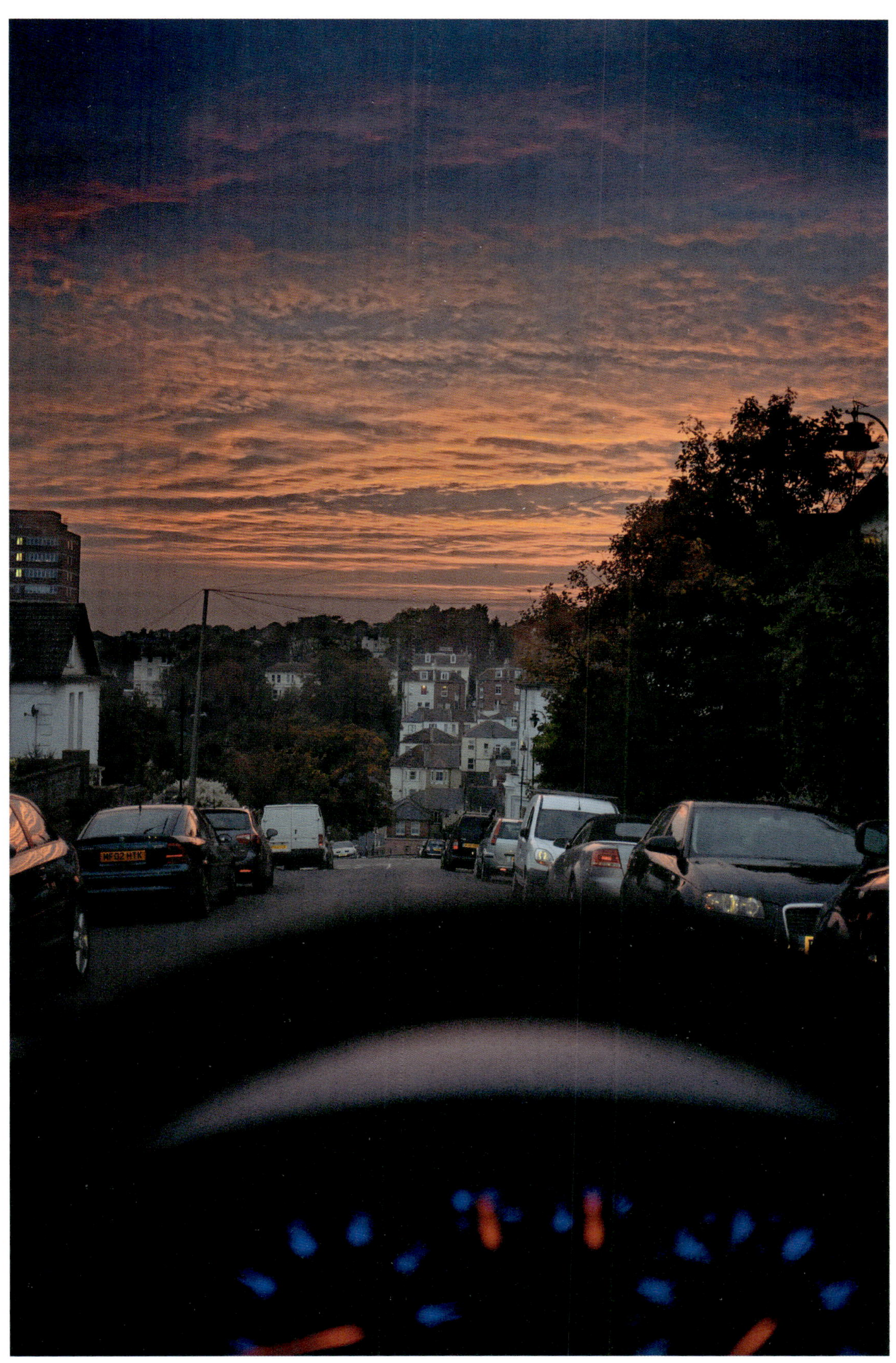

This is a hound. It looks like an evil hound. You don't
want to be where it lands when it lands. I'd been
commissioned to take a picture of the windsurfers –
I'd got the shot lined up. Plenty in shot, all in frame.
Then as I pressed 'shoot' the dog leapt into the picture
out of nowhere.

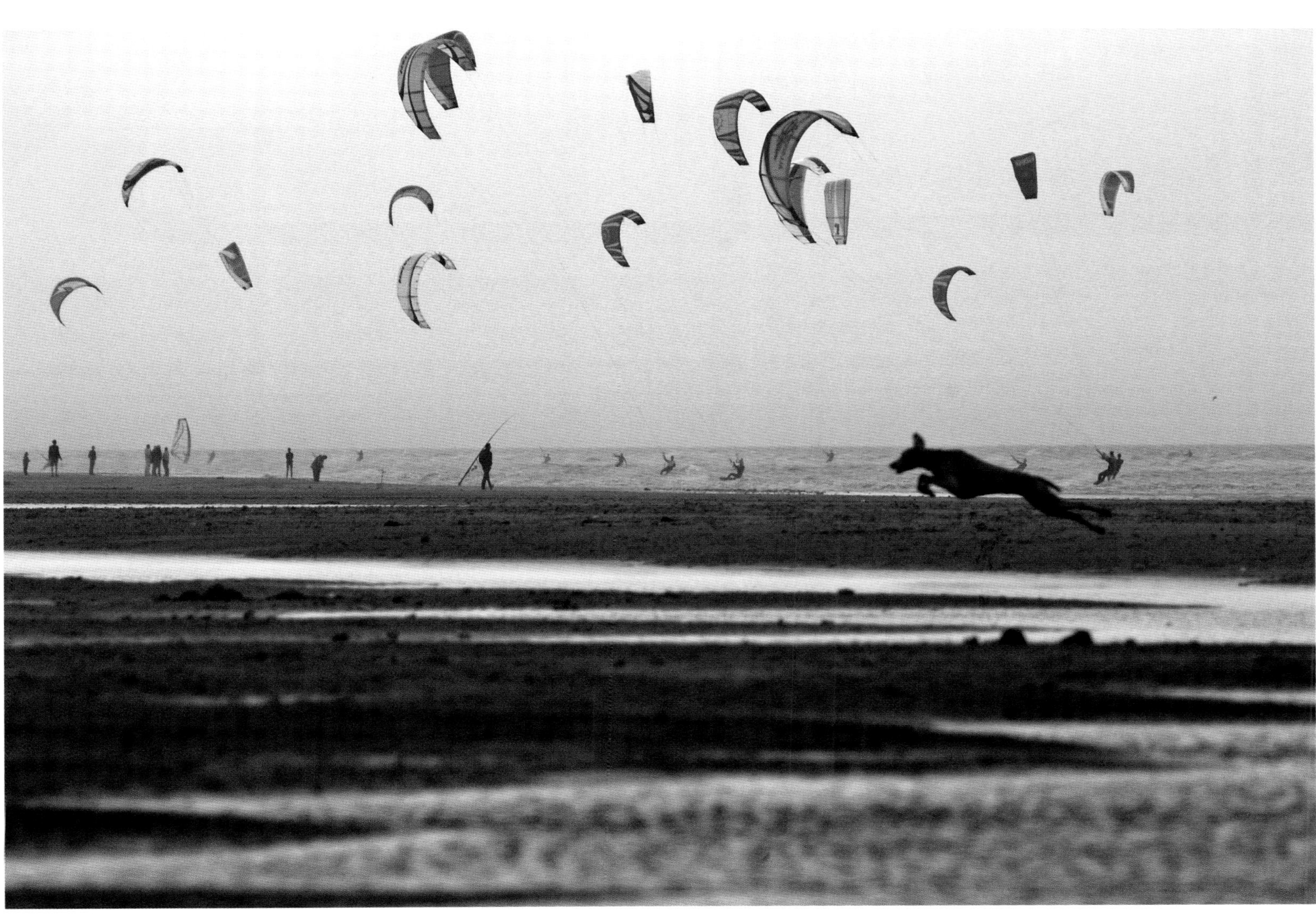

The Mondrian pier.

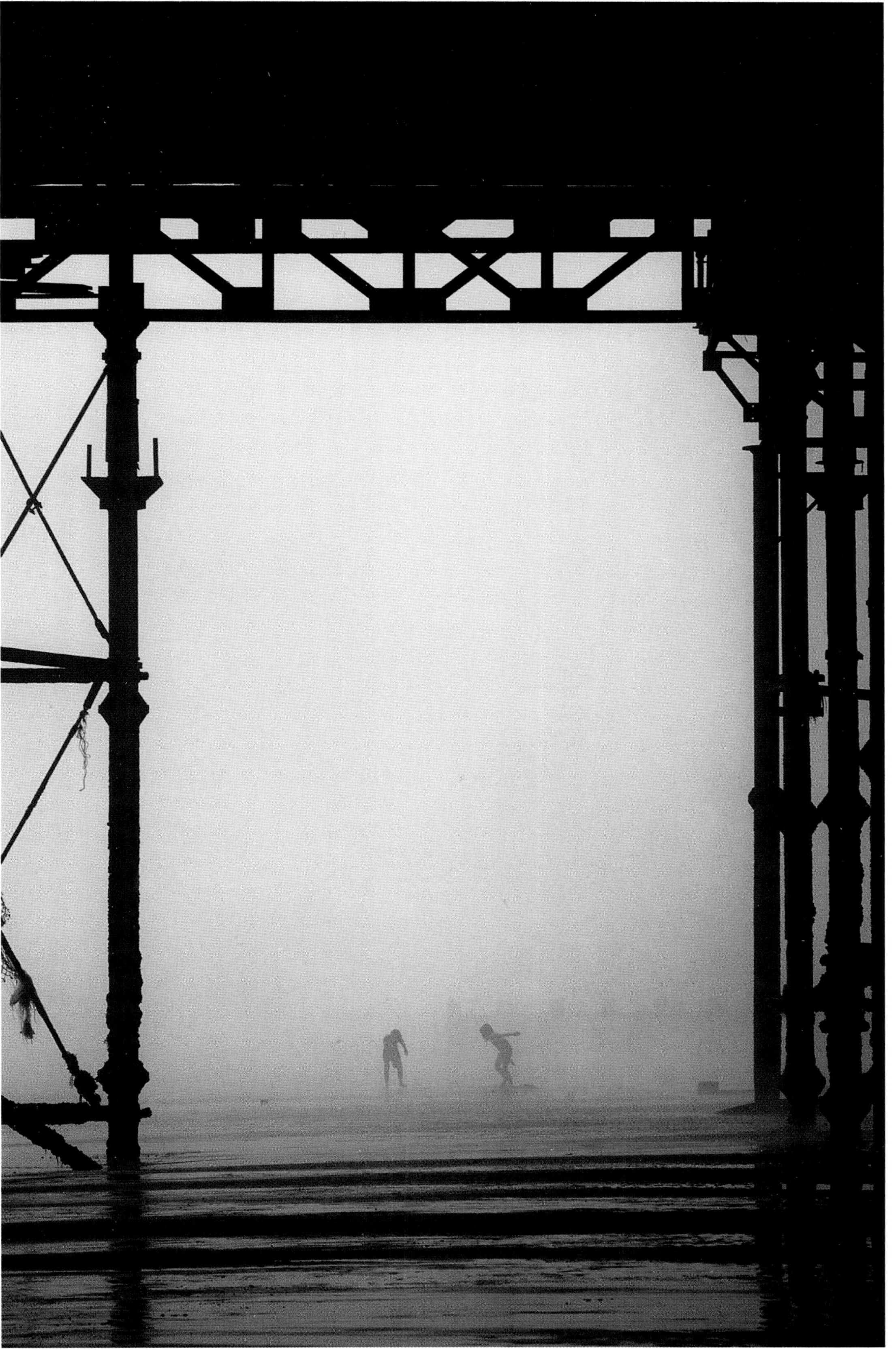

These two remind me of ancient athletes on the isle of
Crete. It's probably a Jean-Luc Goddard and *Le Mépris*
(*The Contempt*) connection. Two amateur boxers on the
seafront by the bathing pool. They'd taken over that
space and it had become the outdoor gym that summer.
But in this particular picture I see them as Cretian
athletes in the Med. Atop a Greek fort.

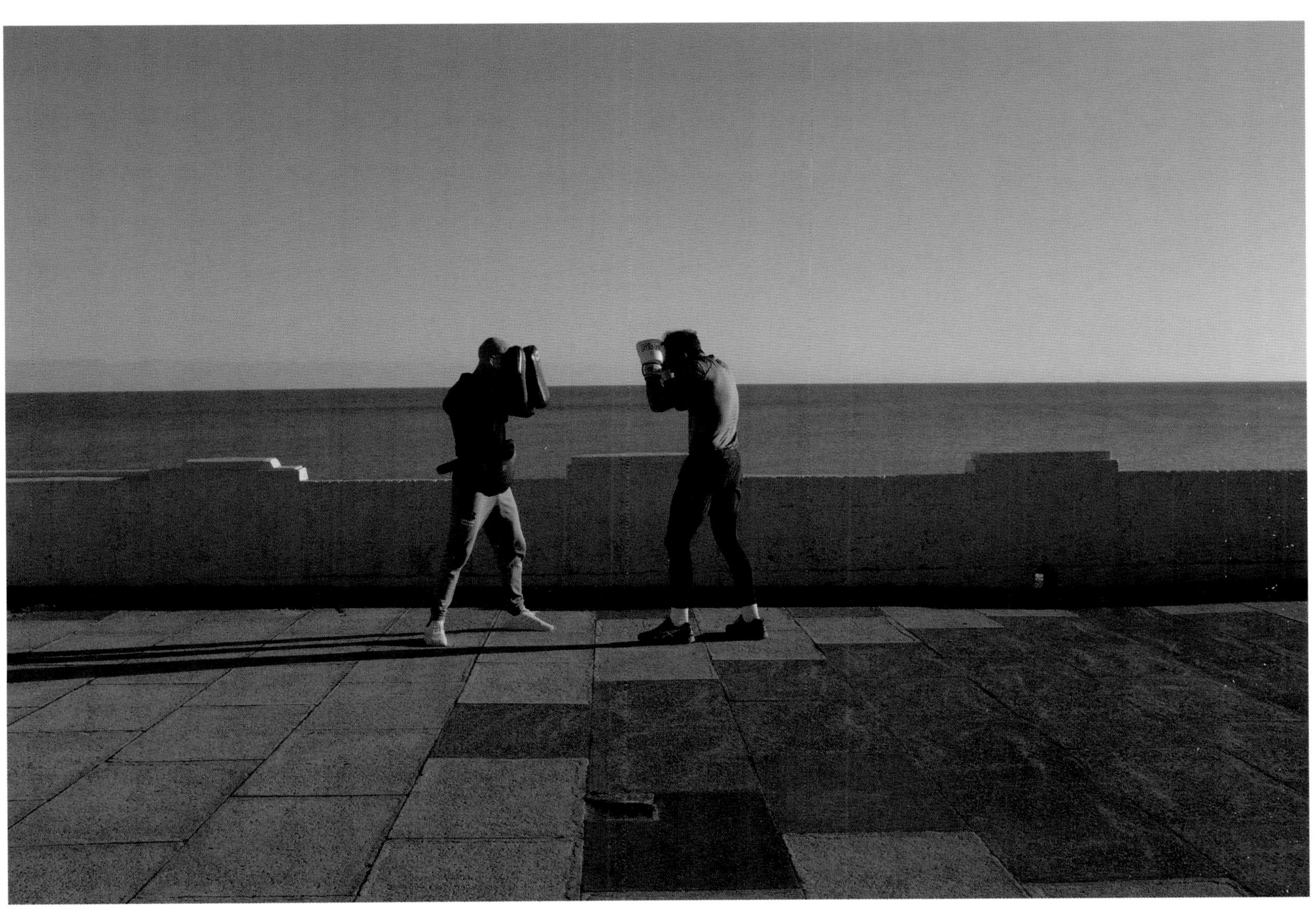

Café with Jen.
A hint of the sun breaking through the clouds – an
optimistic sign to us during the Covid months.

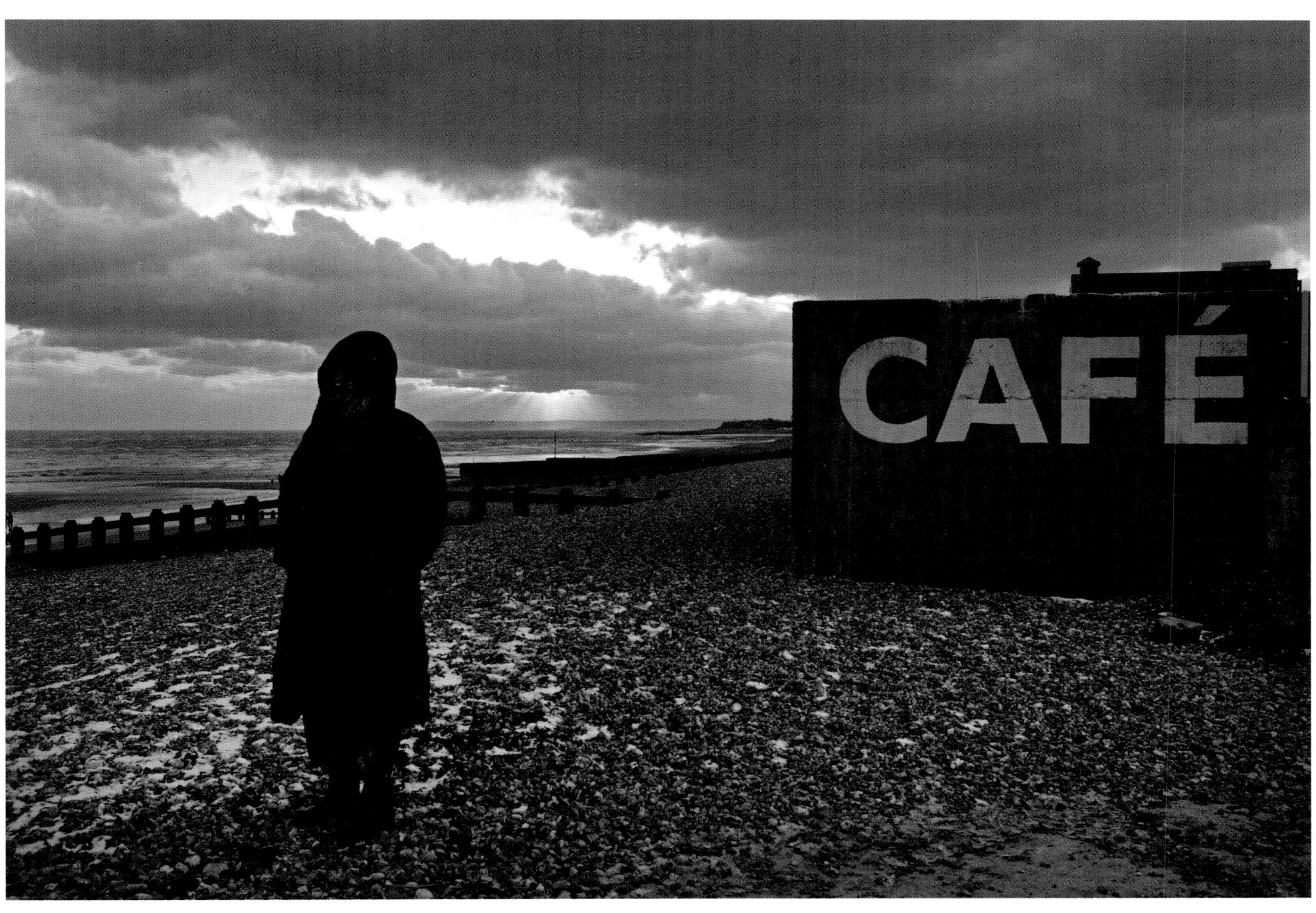
CAFÉ

I met them when photographing a project for the
council. Jamie Oliver was making a Sainsbury's advert
in Hastings, of all places. Tables of yummy food
stretched down the streets and up on to the hillside.
We were on a corner in the Old Town and I thought,
'This must cost an absolute fortune.' And then these
two girls emerged from a nearby house and became
bystanders too. Guess what, I liked the look of them.
What were they doing there? What were they up to
in the house? Would I rather be in the house than out
here photographing Jamie?

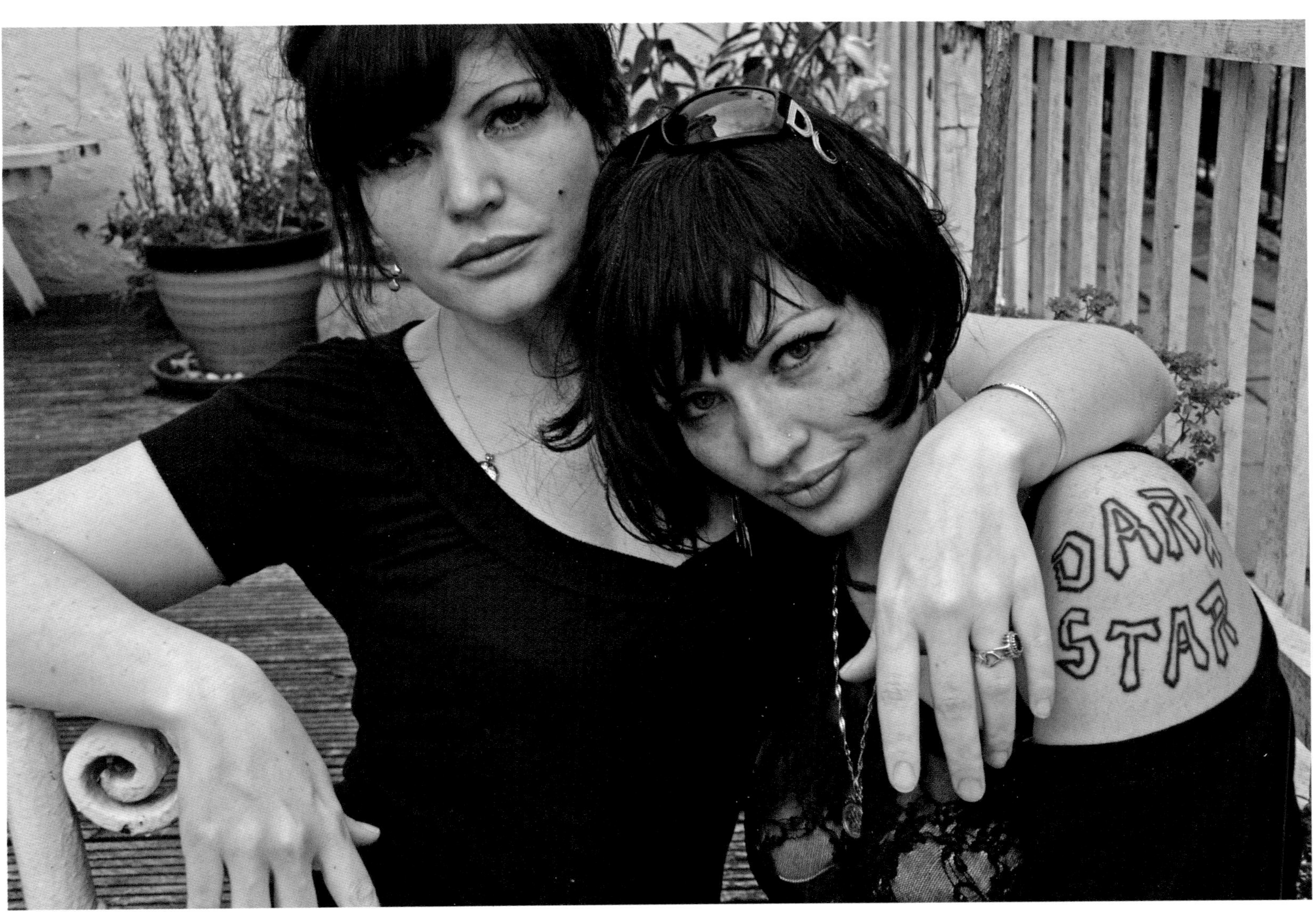
DARK
STAR

I have a sucession of pictures of women giving me
the finger. Just for photographing a kiosk. I liked it in
colour, with the cerise, the moss-coloured roof, the
horizontals and the verticals. Including the vertical
fingers. The vertical finger speaks and moves on.

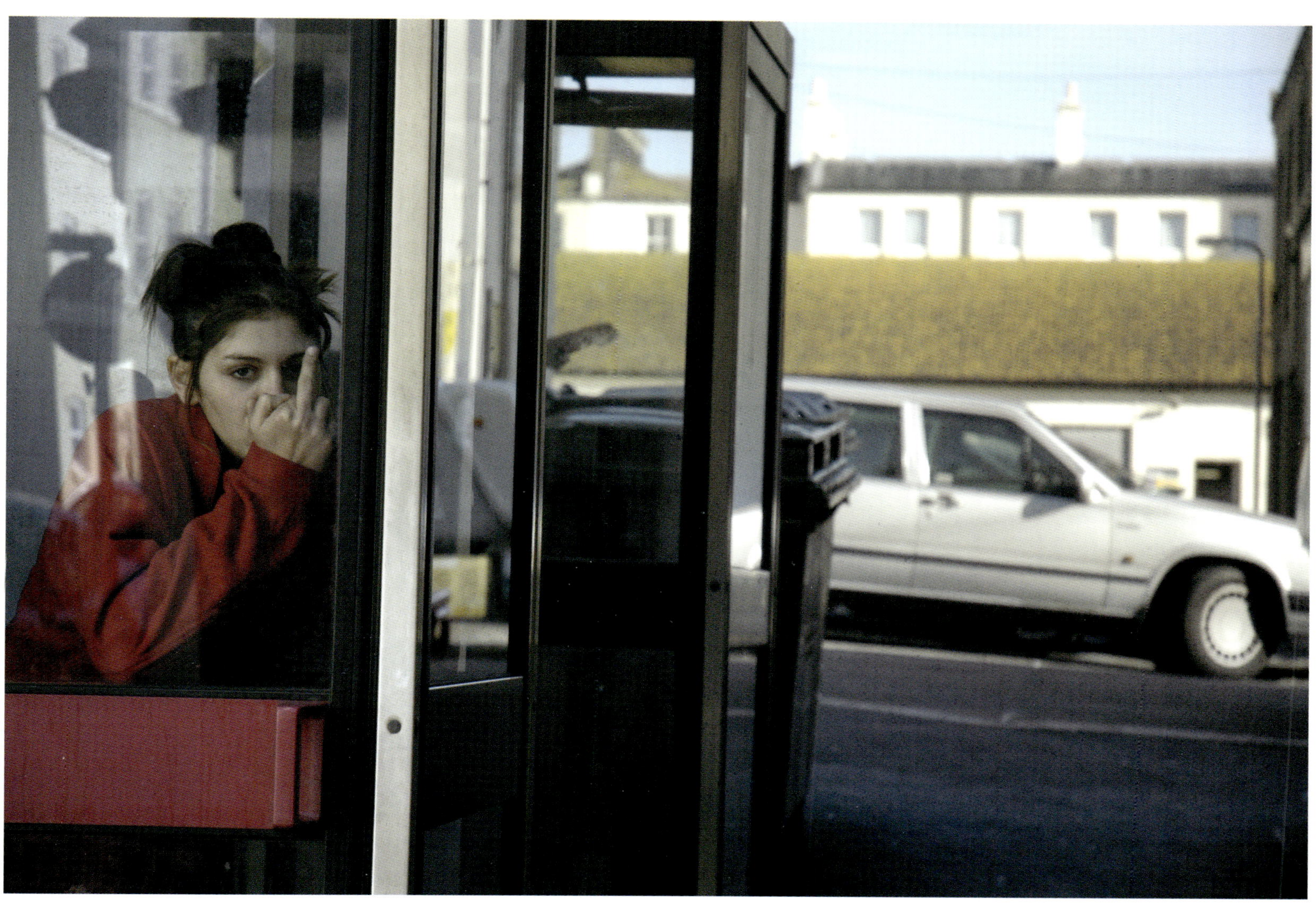

The guy in grey was responsible for the pile of rusty
cars by the flats. A bit of a scary place. All the services
were there. But they shut this guy down – I presume
that's his family looking through the window. The
little boy looks like he is troubled – it made me think
of the social life of these people.

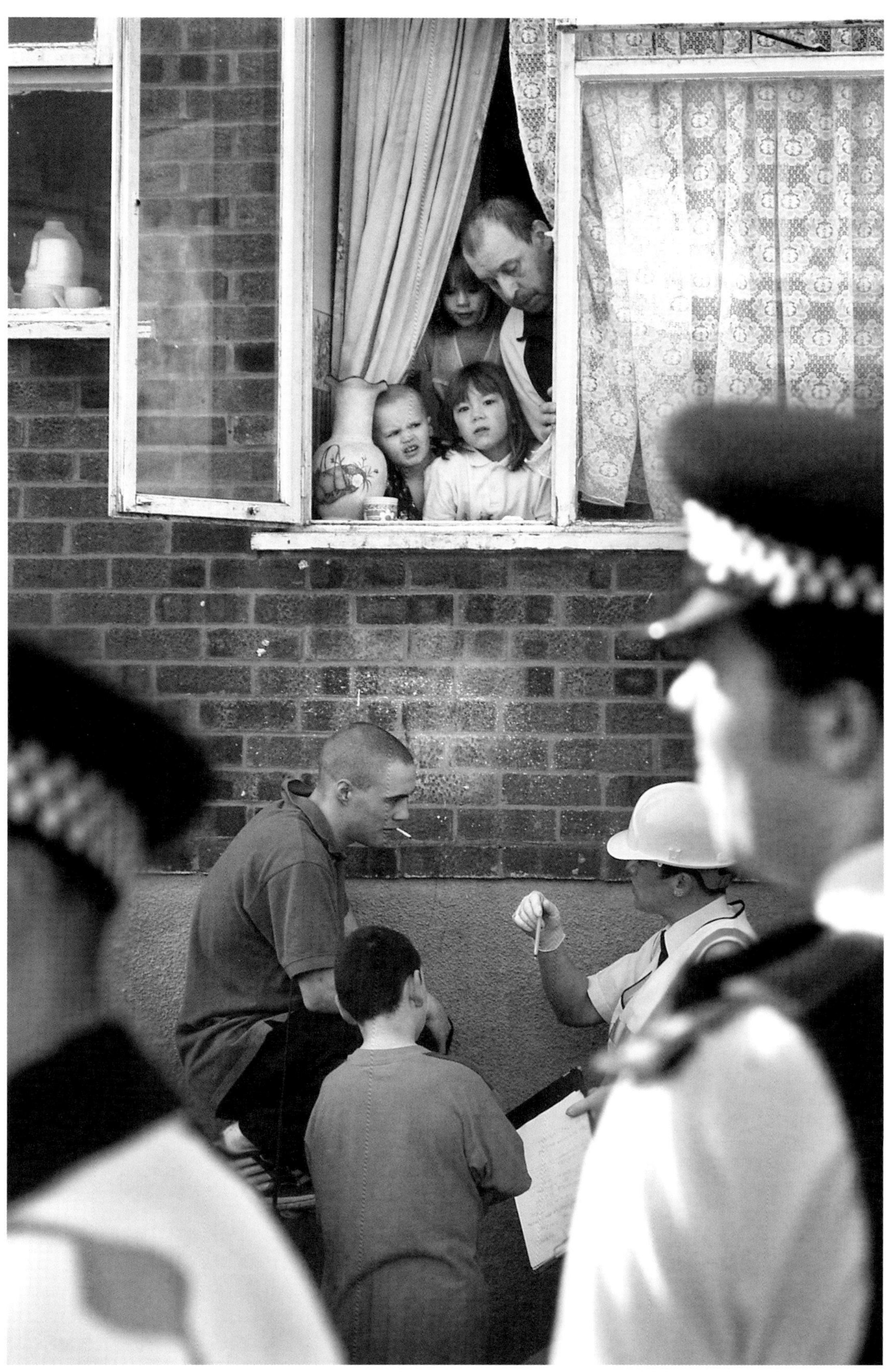

Woman sitting on pavement. A drive-by shot.
And I wasn't driving for a change.

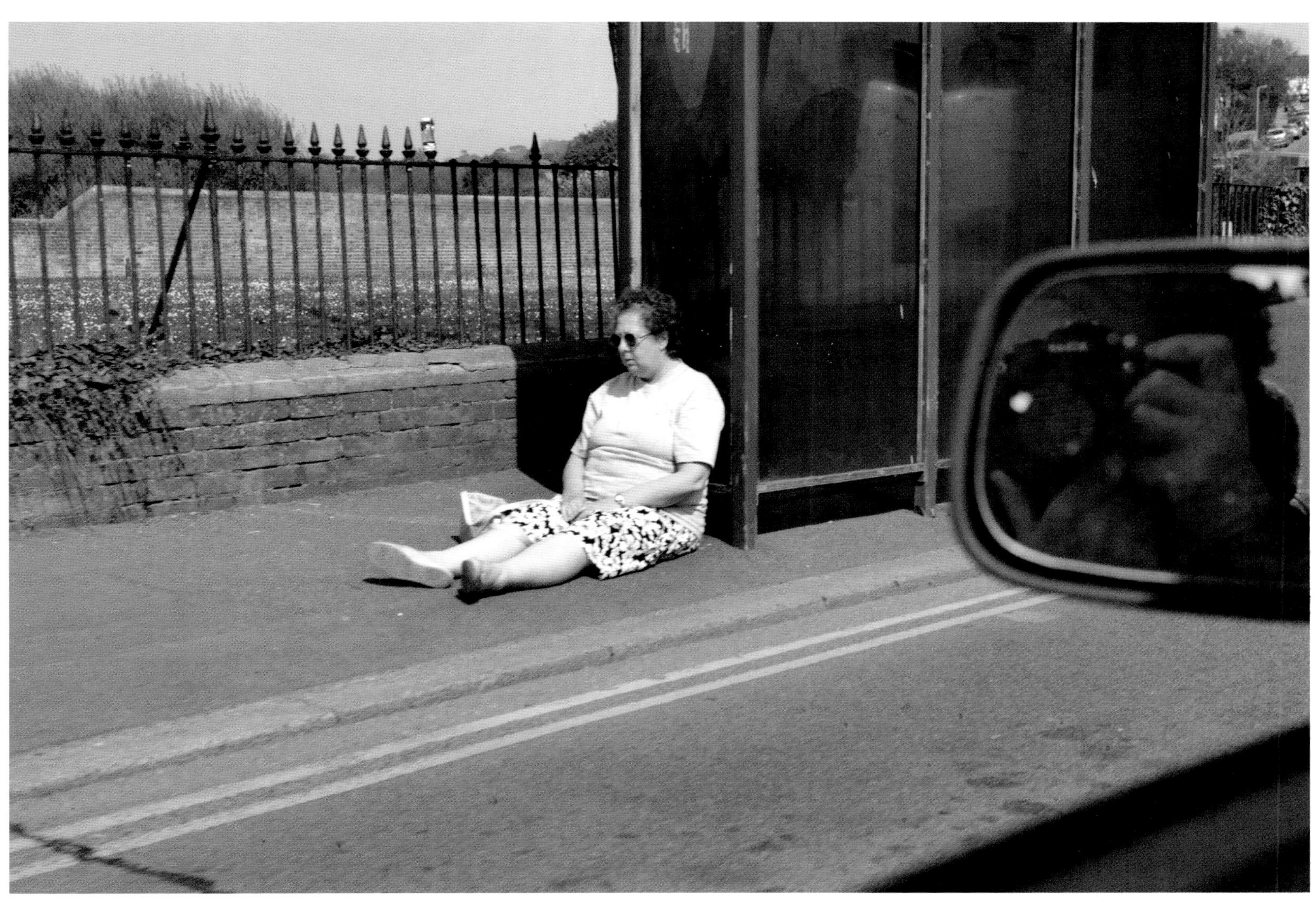

A St Leonards' kind of humour.

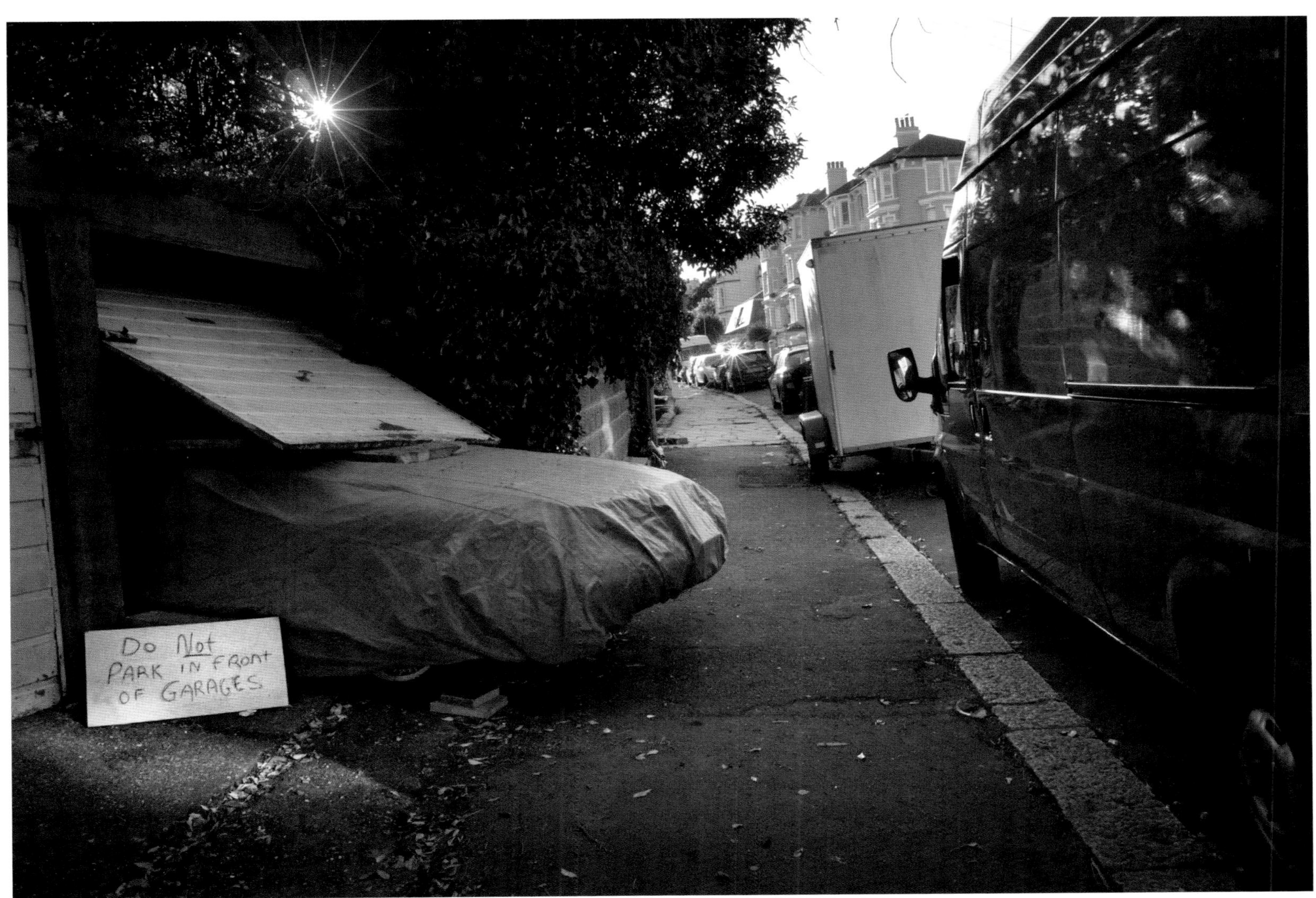
Do Not
PARK IN FRONT
OF GARAGES

Partly a commissioned shot near Rye, to photograph
a farm, but then I'd gone off to wander around the
countryside. I saw this cloud bubbling up on the
horizon, almost like a cloud monster. So I quickly
put on my fisheye lens, then I held the camera upside
down so the flash lit up the reeds right in front of me.

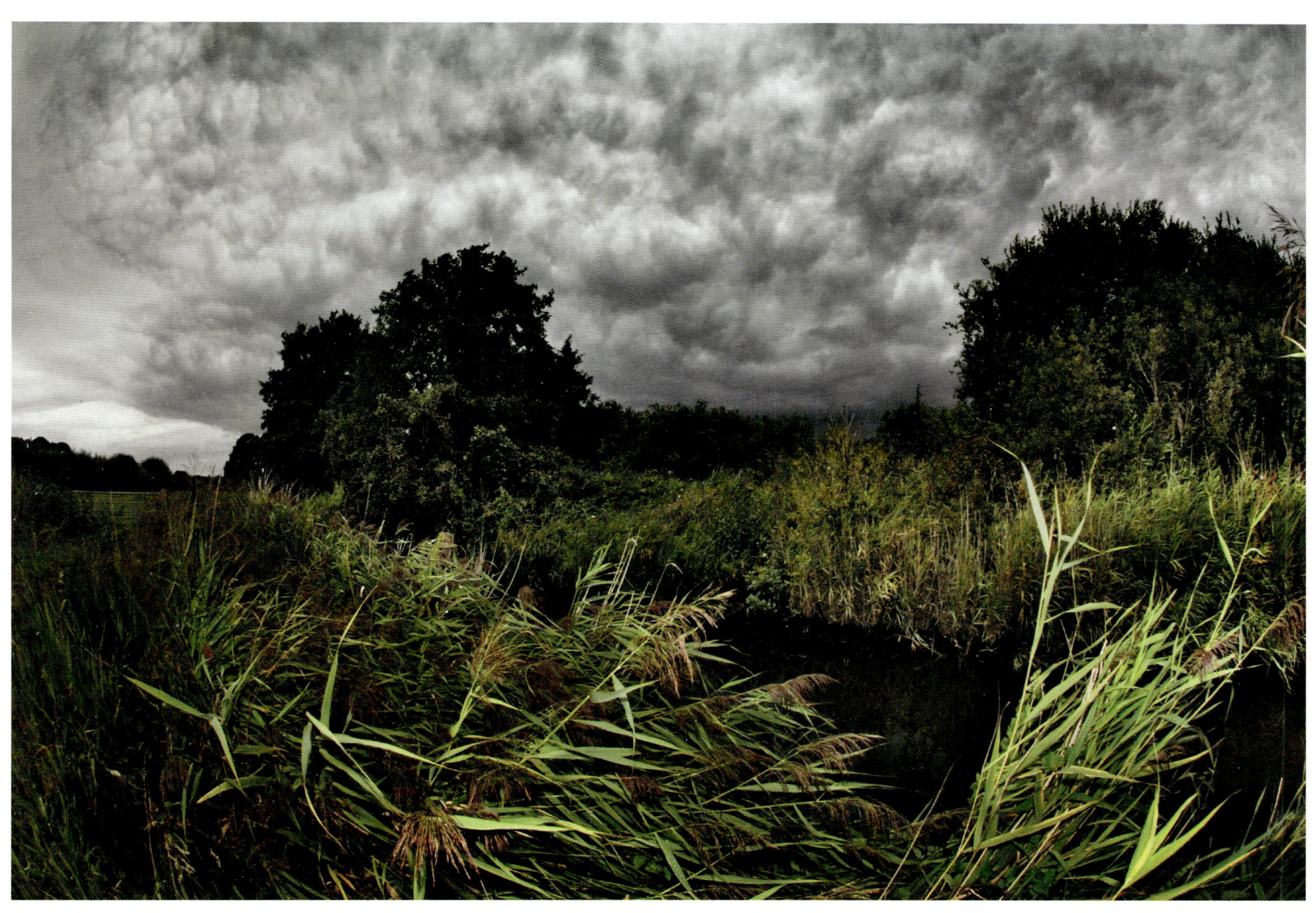

On the right side of the canal that goes
down to the sea at Rye. The Nature Reserve.

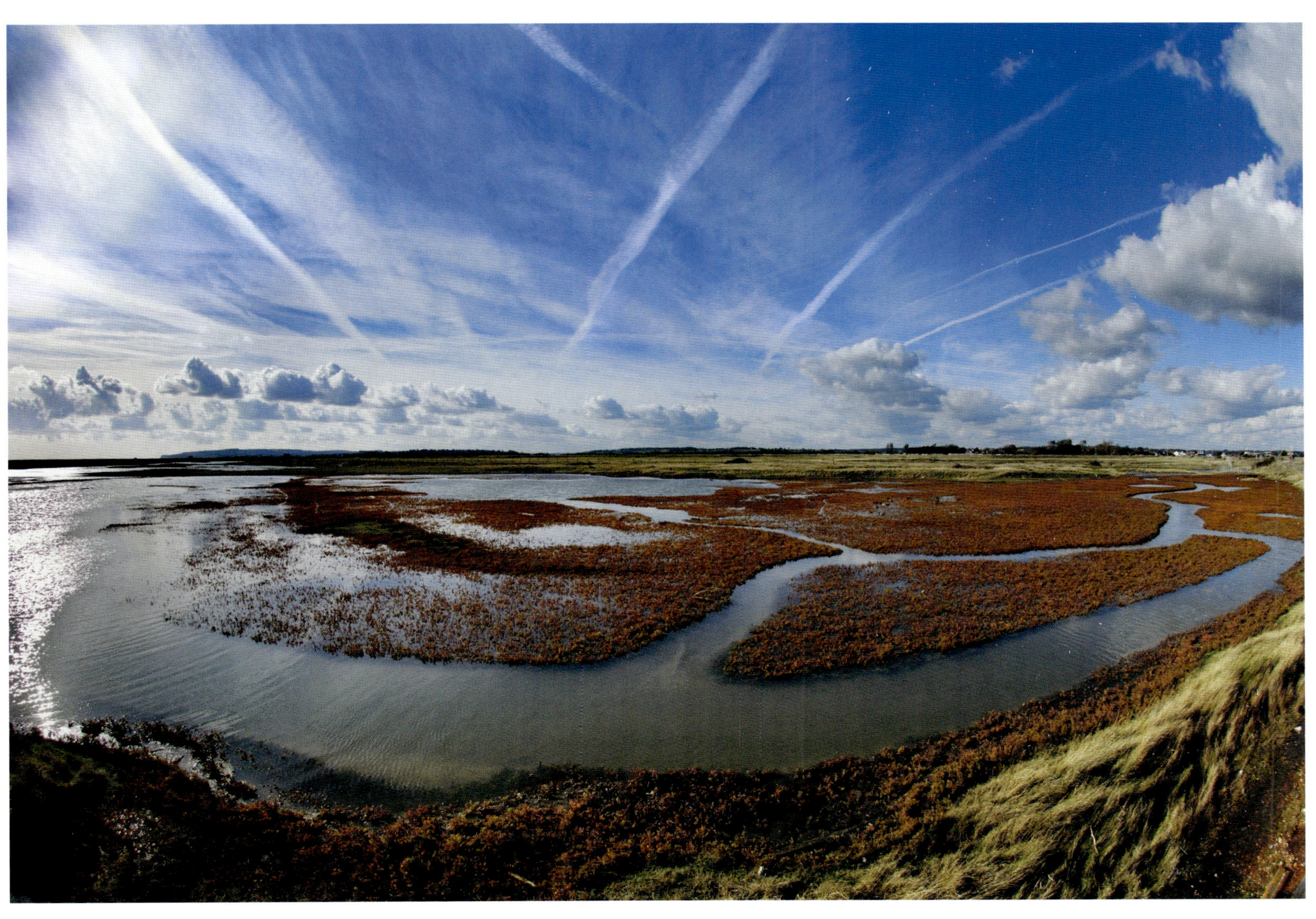

Someone I know who goes swimming towing a little
packet with his clothes in, so he can swim a long
distance and then get dressed wherever and whenever
he lands. I think he's an actor. It looks like I'm in the
water with him but I wasn't.

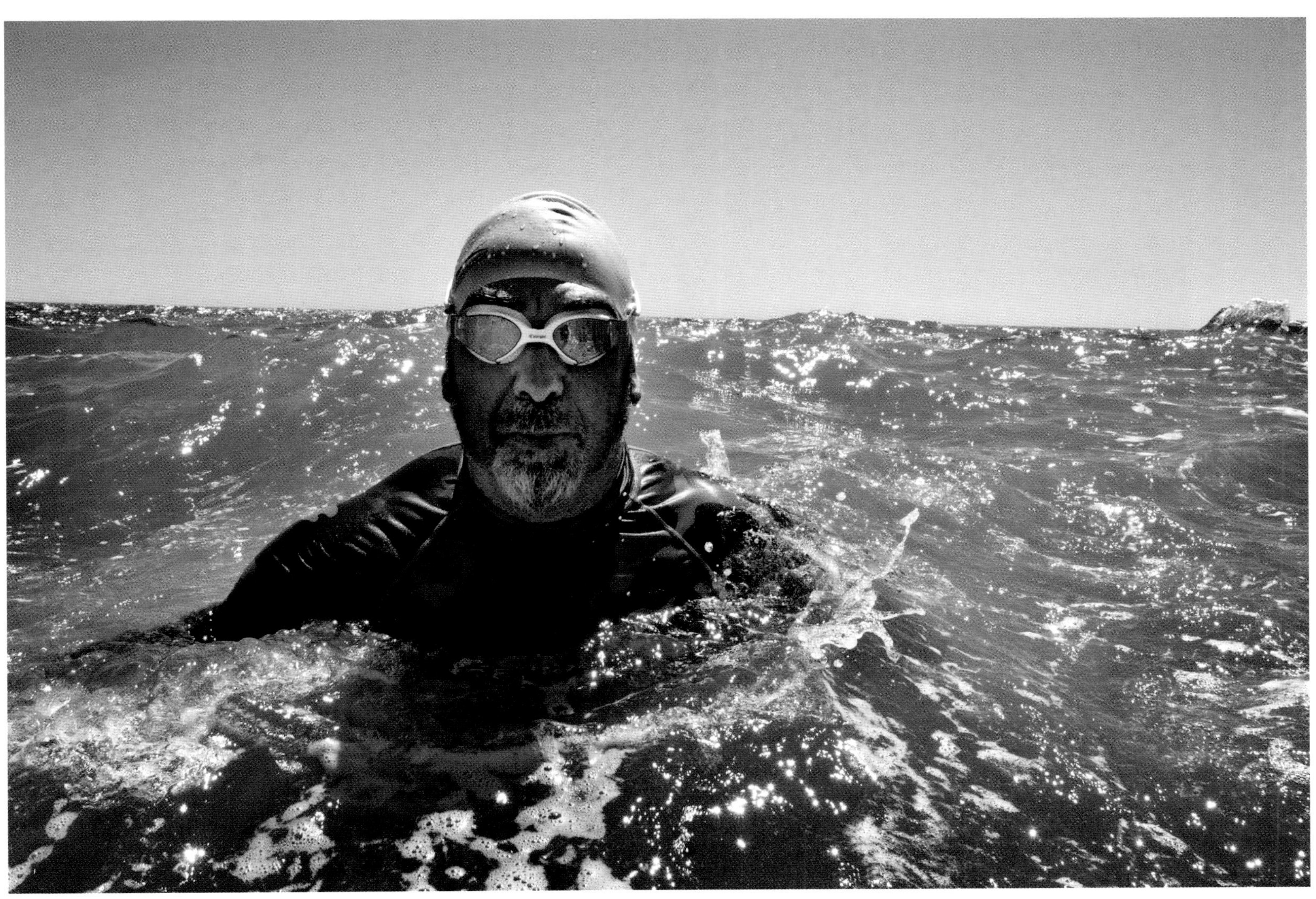

Bodybuilders on the old pier when there used to be
a competition every year. There is a touch of sadness
about this picture. Tyrone, the second guy from the
left, one day just collapsed on the street and died.

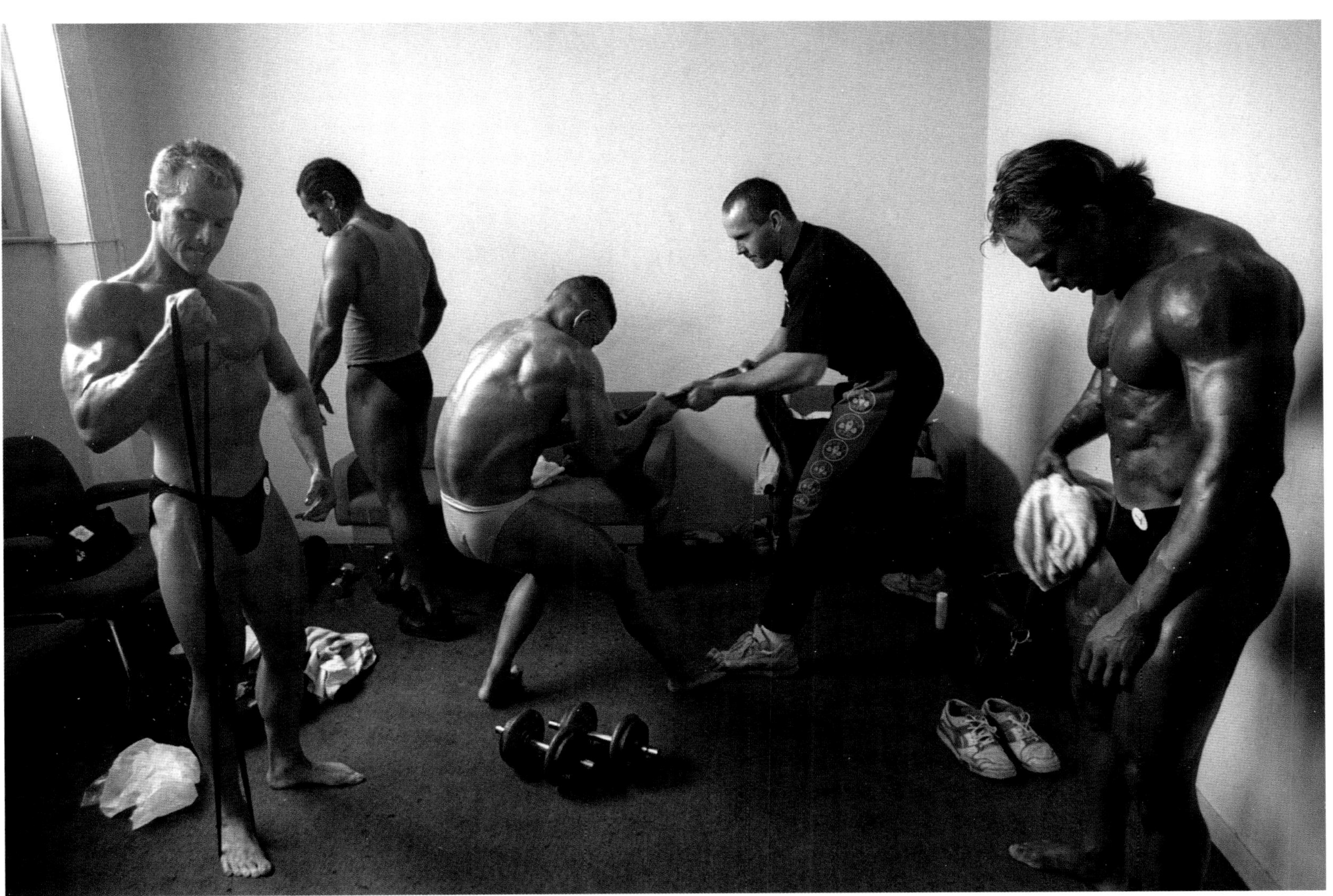

Local breadmaker in the Old Town.
Photographed for a book about food.

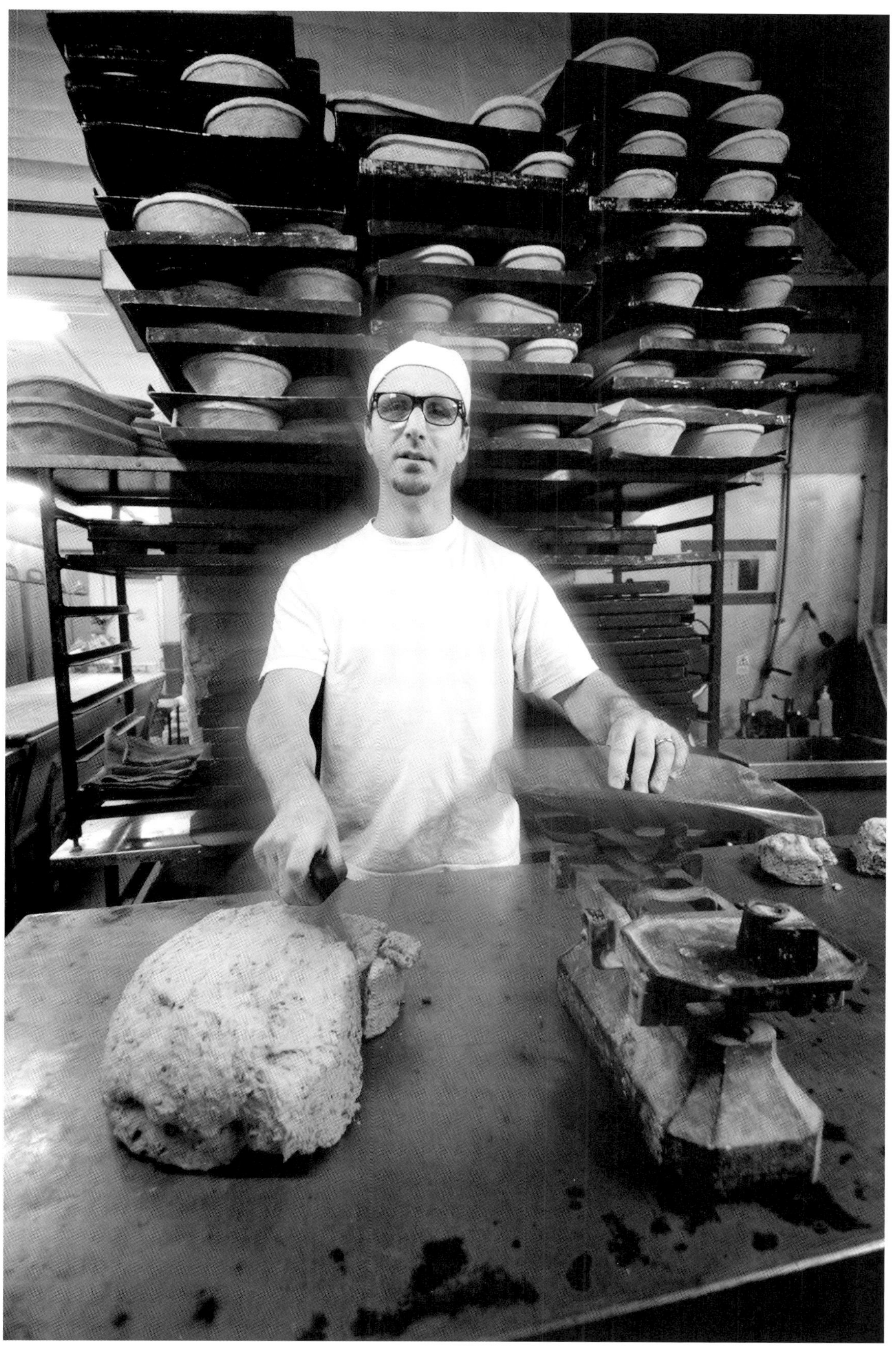

A picture for the local newspaper. I would be sent at
weekends to endless jumble sales. Just complete fun.

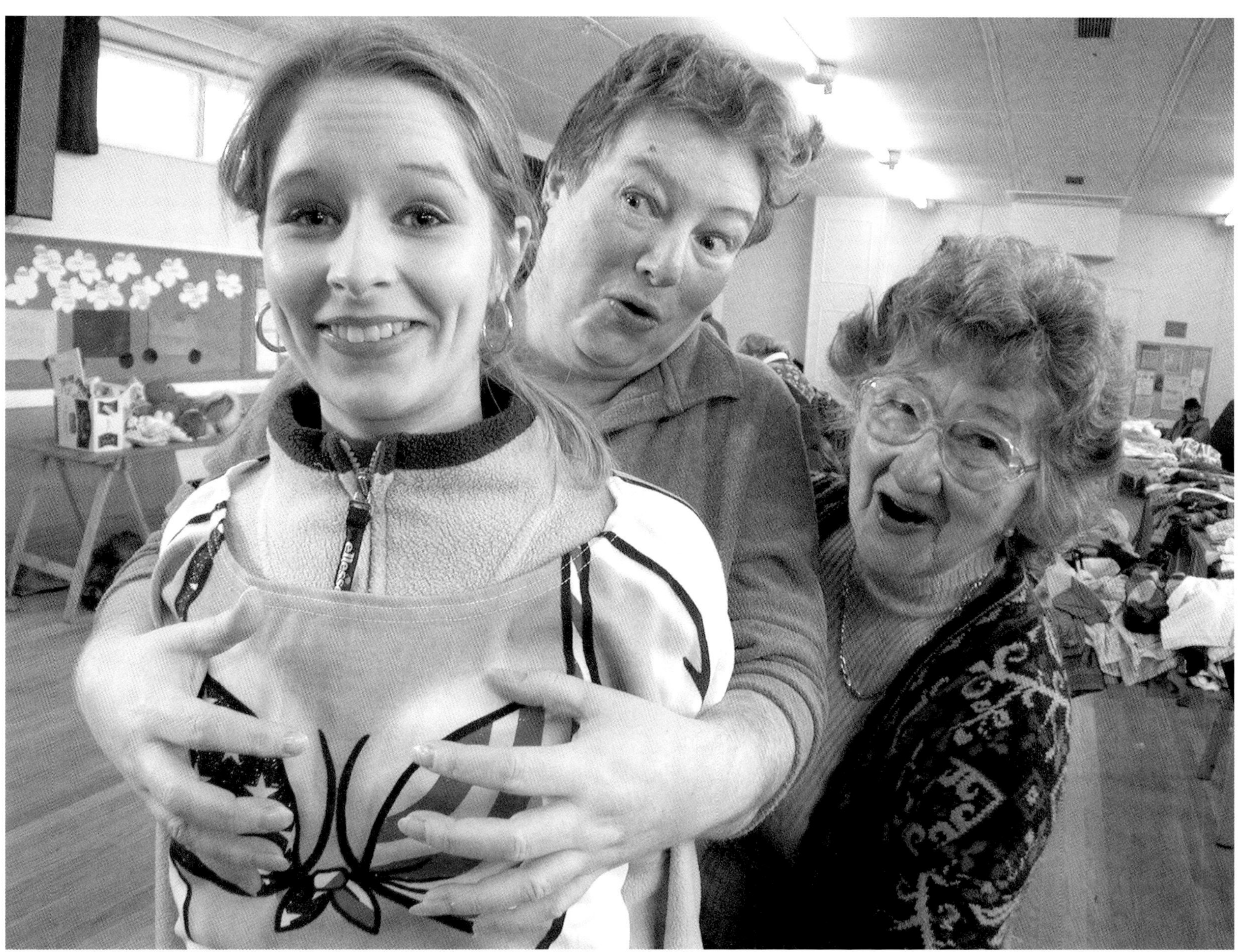

A festival in the Old Town. A moving picture.

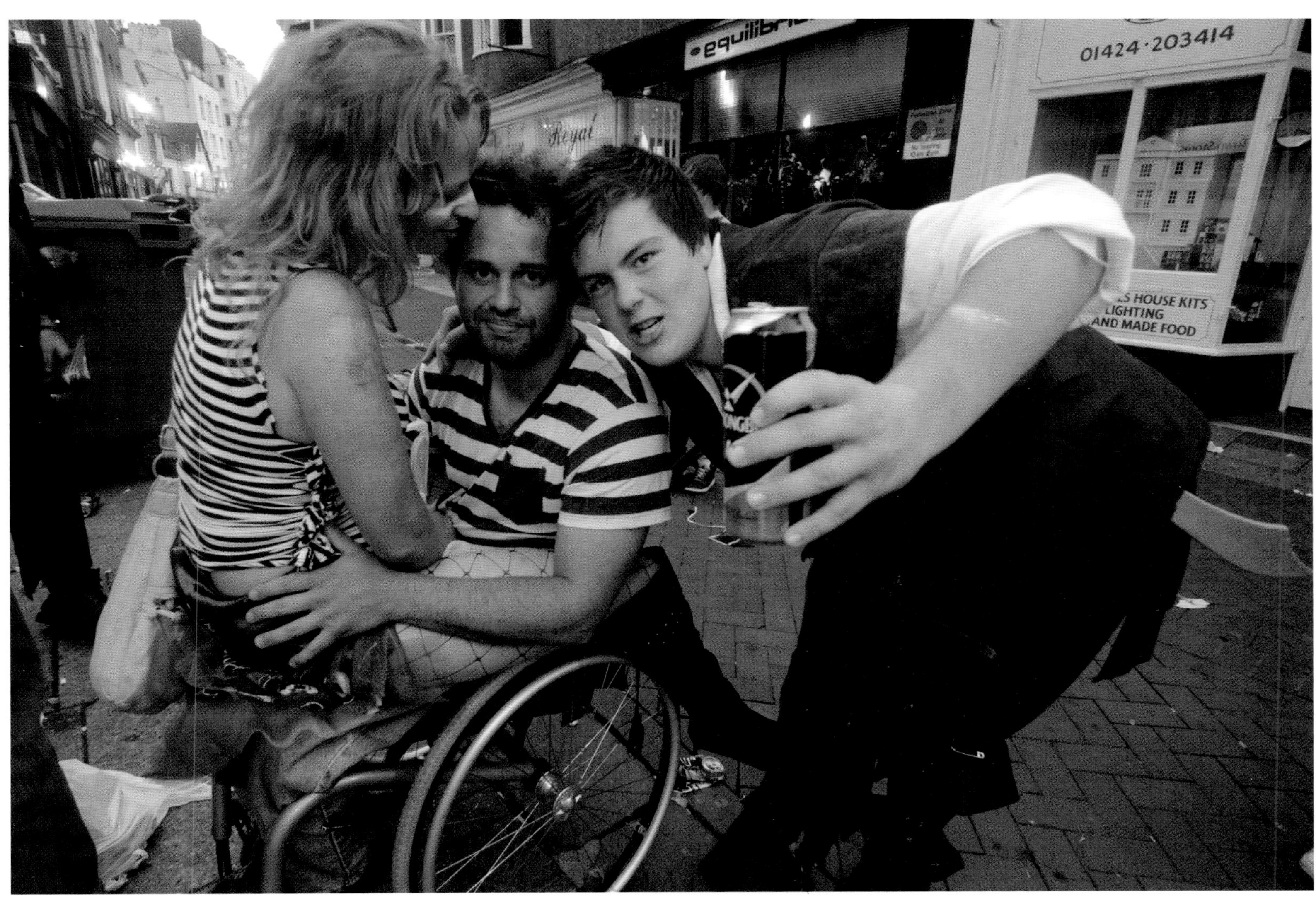

equilibri
01424·203414
S HOUSE KITS
LIGHTING
AND MADE FOOD
Royal

Snake in St Leonards. Perfectly normal.

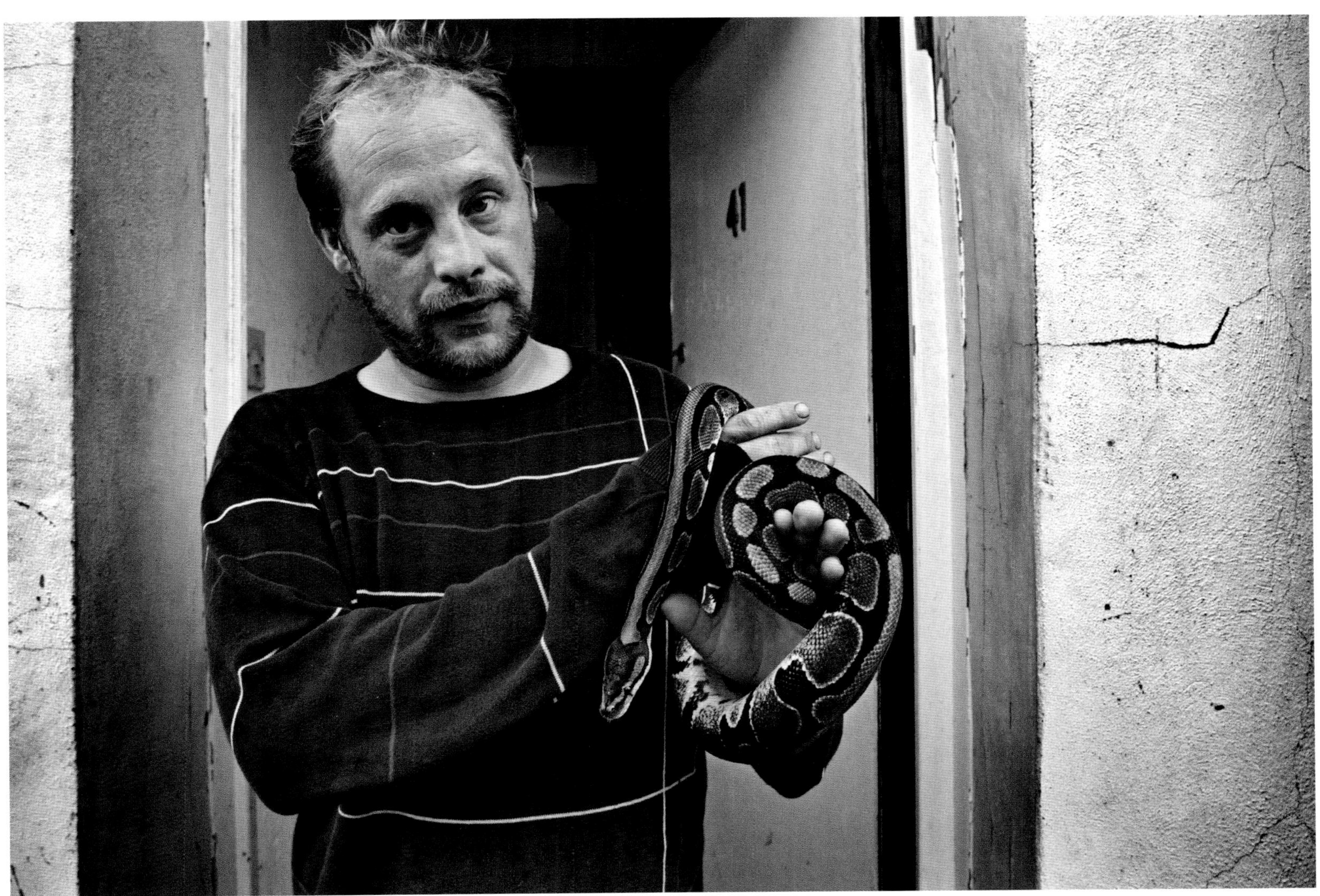

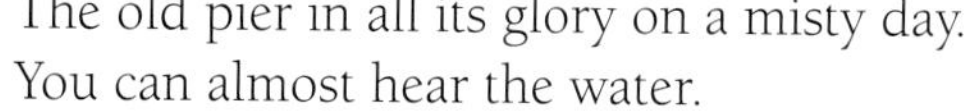

The old pier in all its glory on a misty day.
You can almost hear the water.

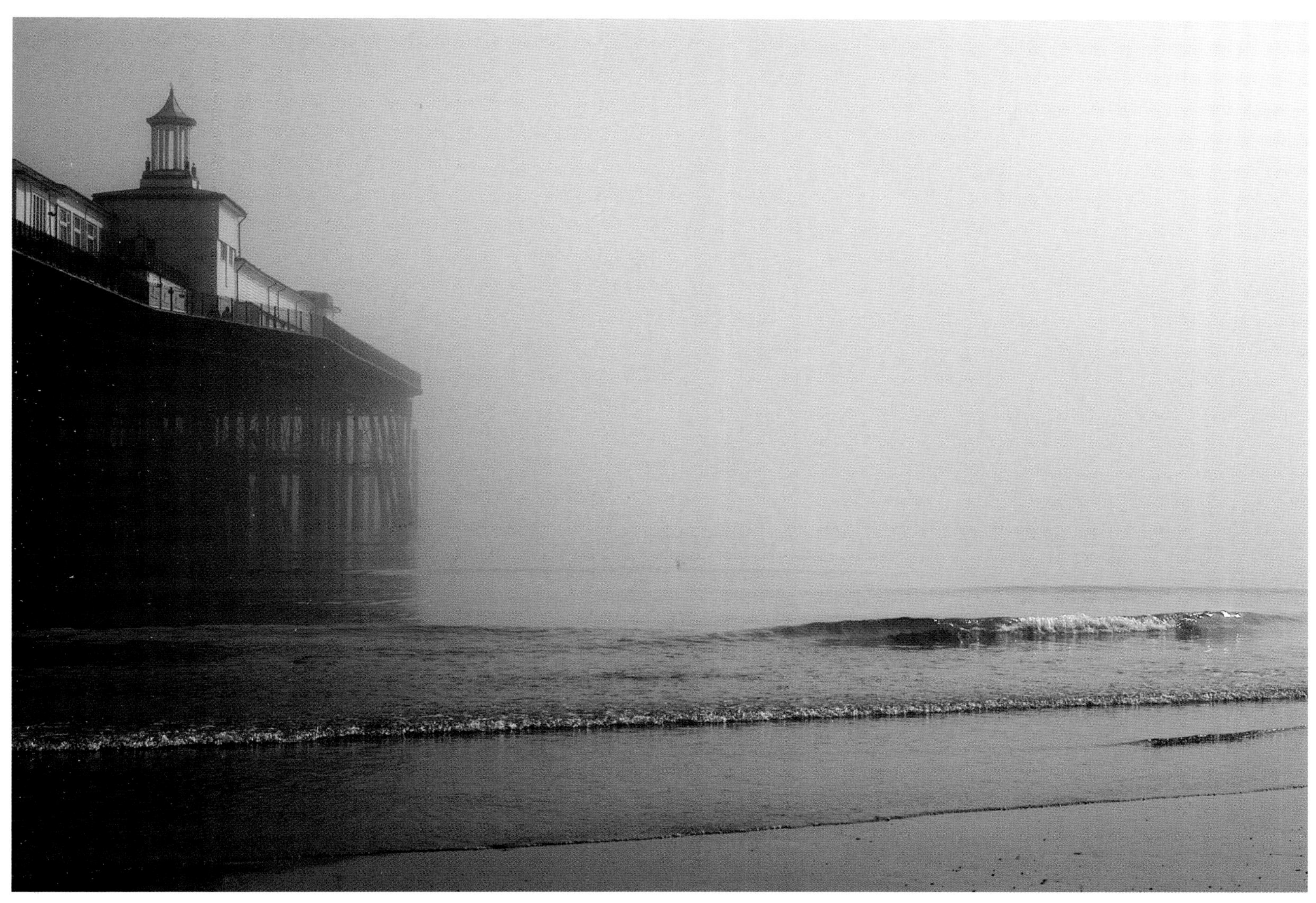

I was at that café in Bexhill – Sovereign Light Café –
and the bird was being fed chips.

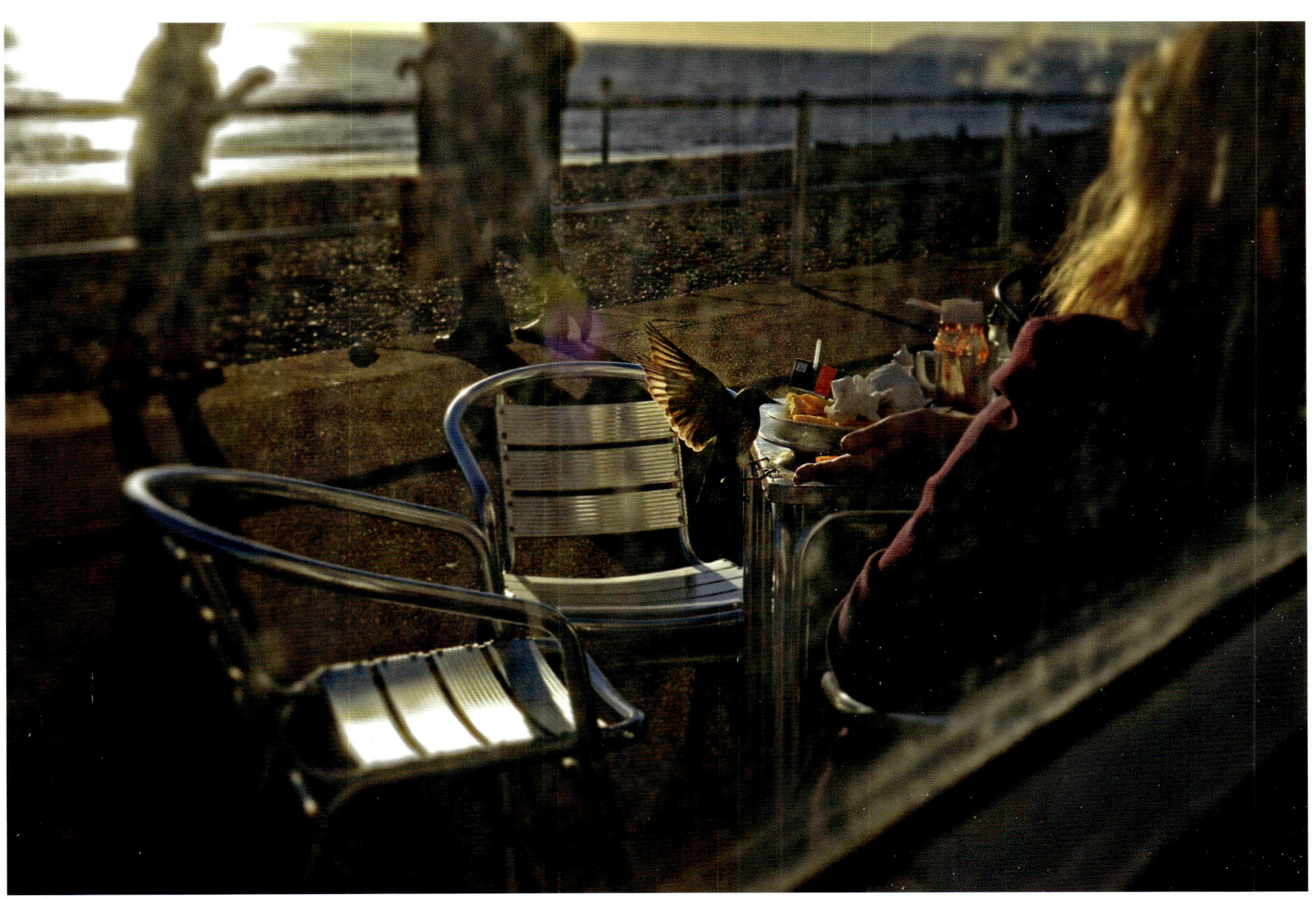

Mysterious couple at a window. That was a hard
picture to take because I didn't want to get beaten up
for it. They either didn't notice me or didn't mind.

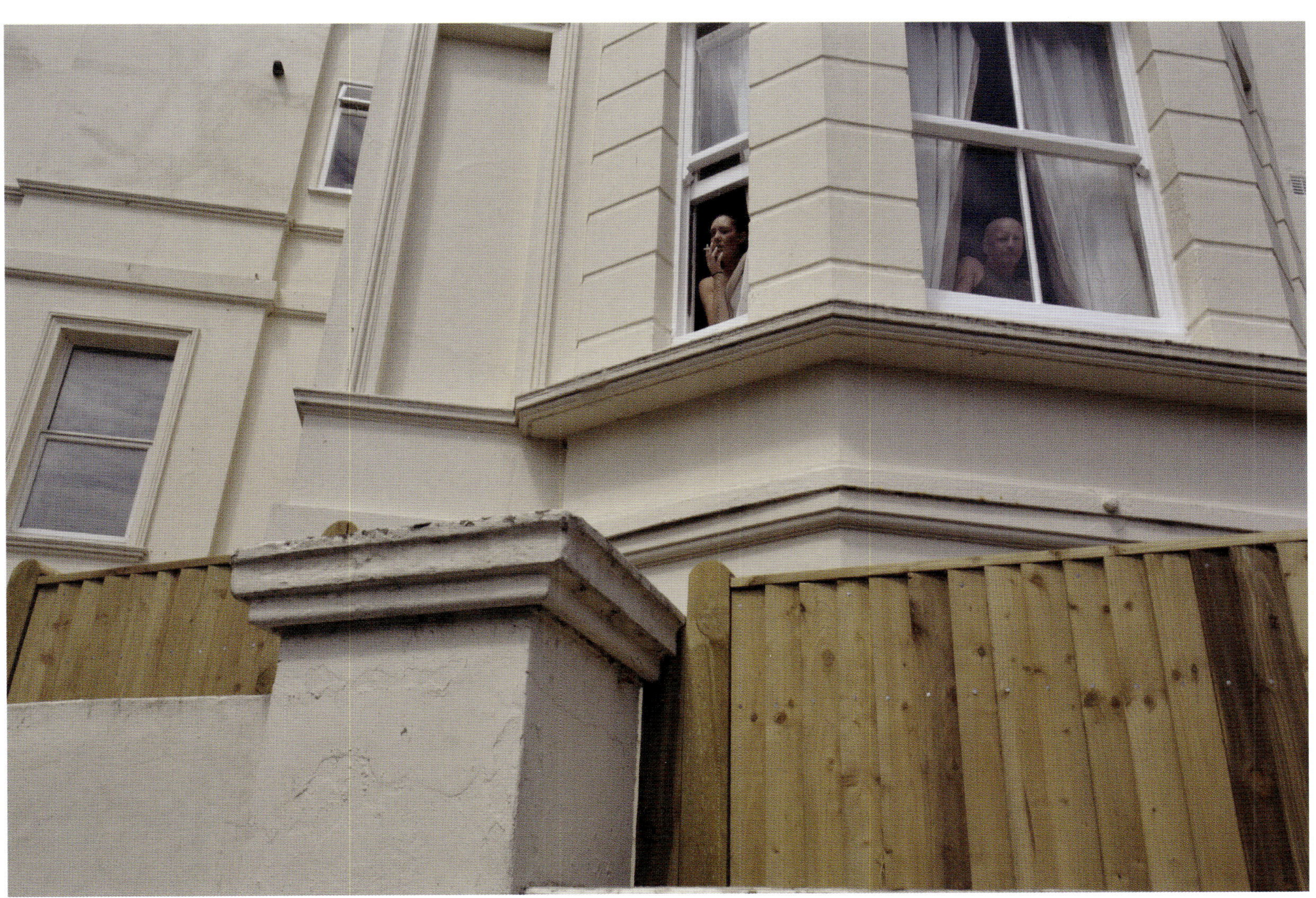

Len and Angie's rainbow.
They both died within weeks of each other. Both
had cancer and I'd photographed their marriage only
weeks before. This is where they had lived.

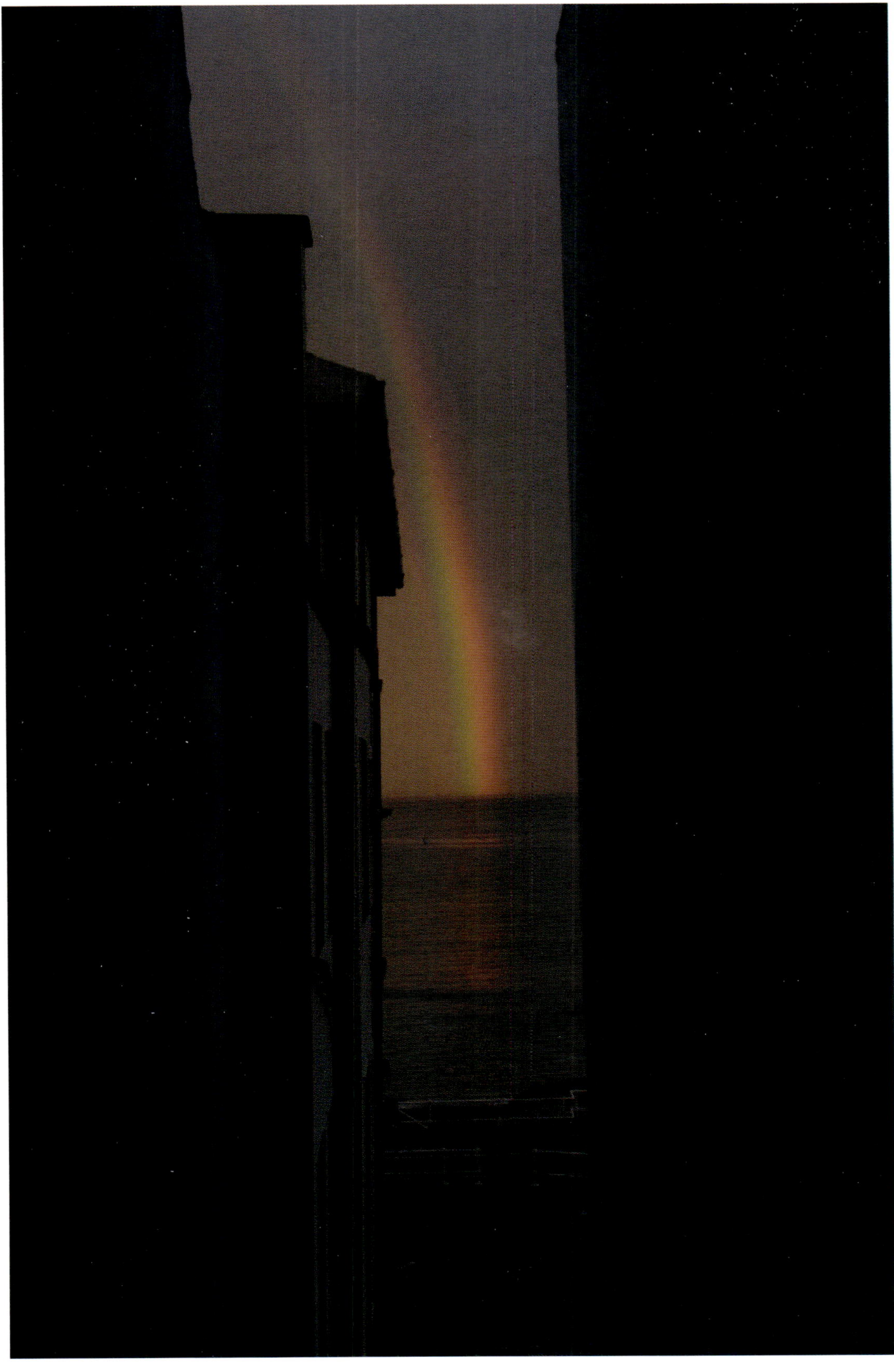

A perfectly useable kitchen unit.
Just chucked out. A drive-by shot.

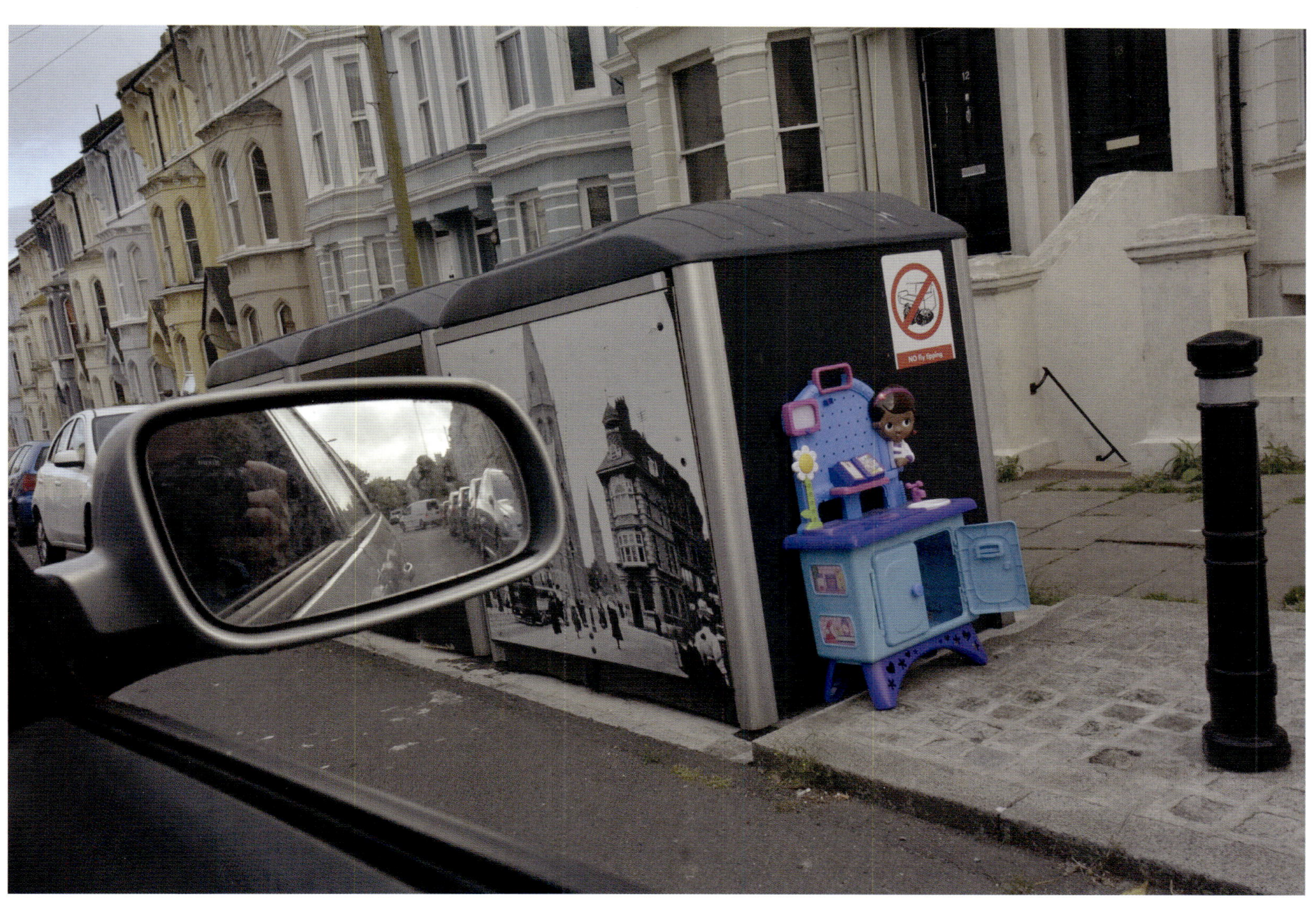
NO fly tipping

The sisters. I kept bumping into them here and there.
This is the best shot I had of them. They were very
used to being photographed.

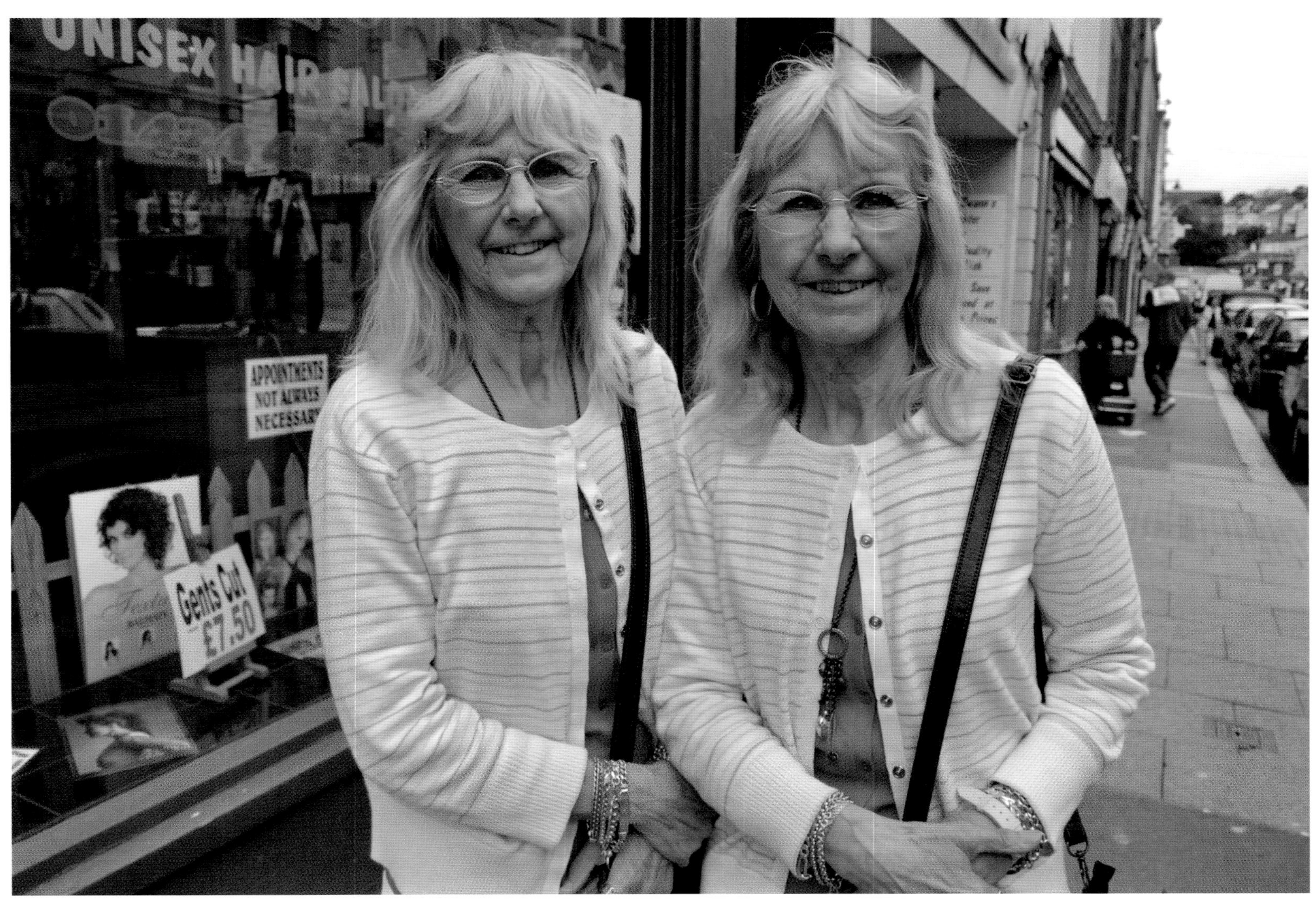
UNISEX HAIR
APPOINTMENTS
NOT ALWAYS
NECESSARY
Gents Cut
£7.50

Pablo – Mr Good Vibes.
When he was around I just felt all right. He and his
wife ran a very useful club for disaffected youths.
As soon as the kids entered through the door they
were transformed into good citizens. I spent a year
and a half photographing them. This was the first
shot I took of the whole project.

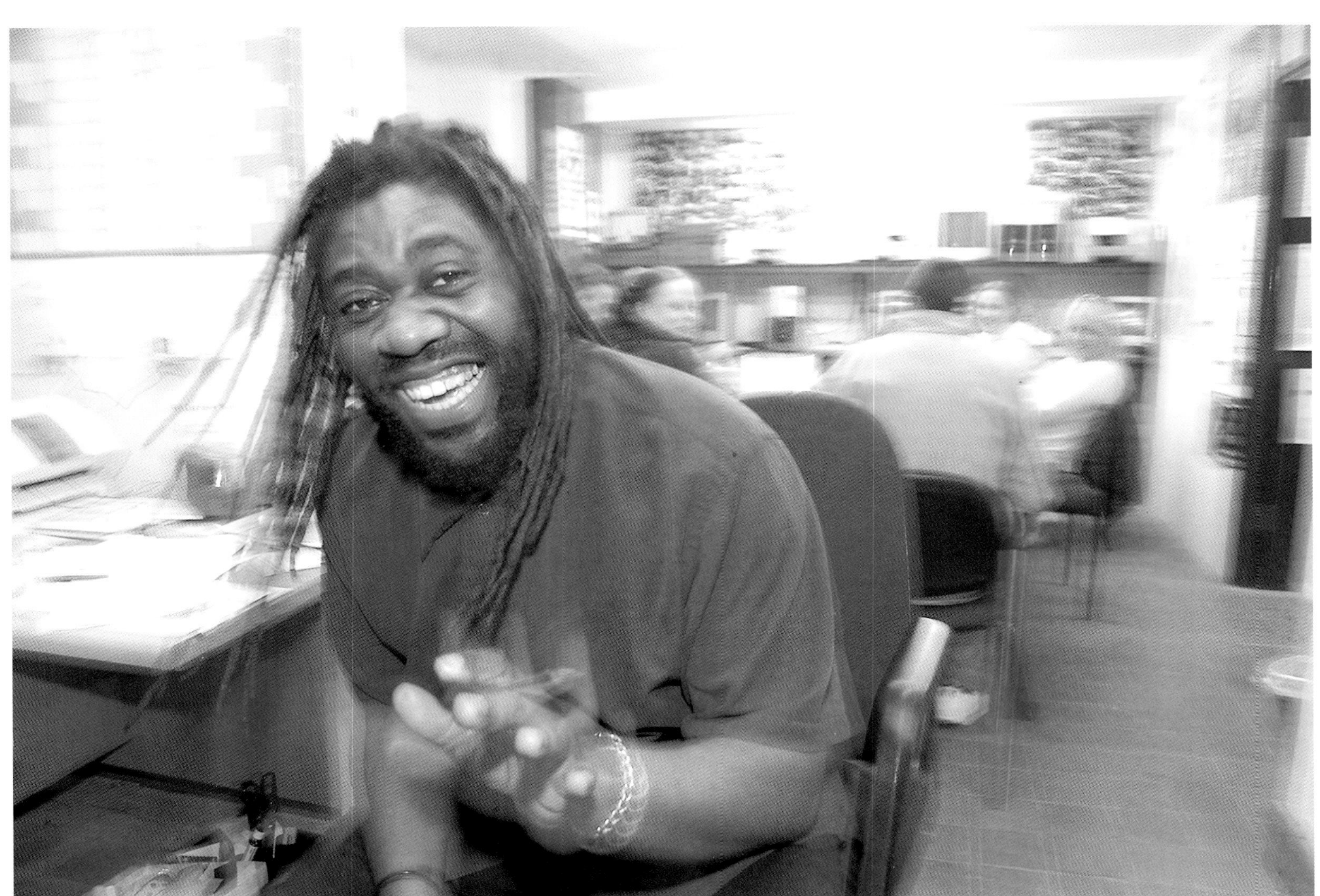

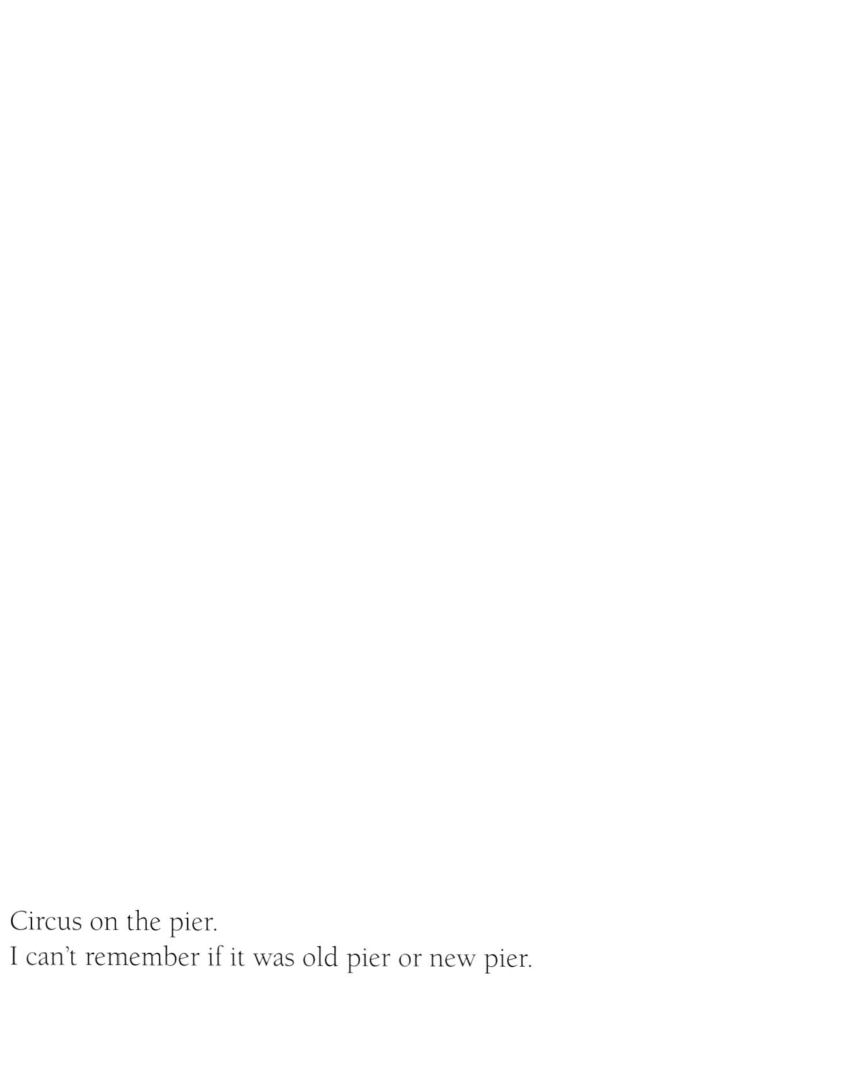

Circus on the pier.
I can't remember if it was old pier or new pier.

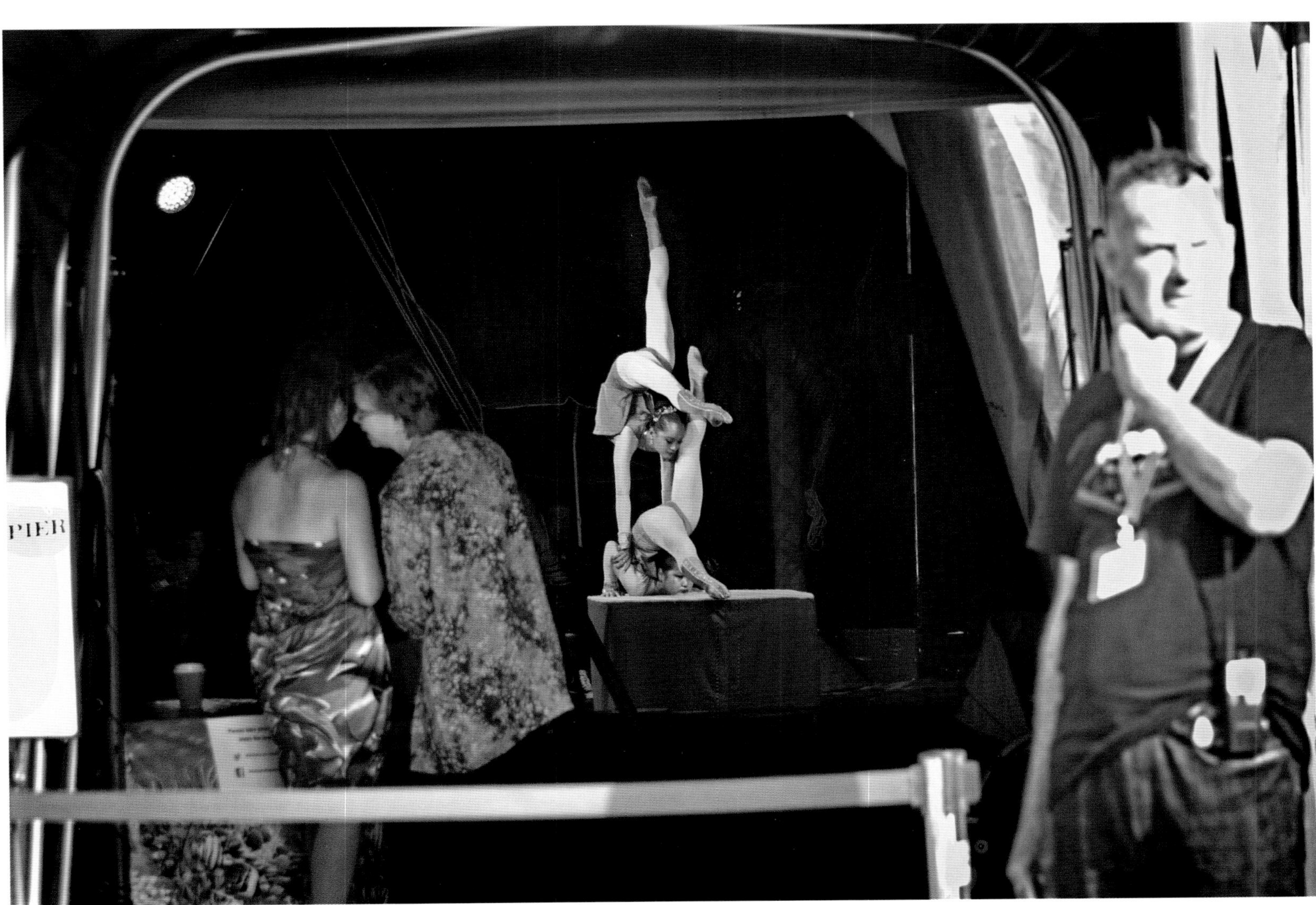

Another Covid picture.
I'm obviously standing outside, but when I first saw
this couple I was driving by and stopped at the lights.
I had to drive on. I parked, walked back down and
tried to take a surreptitious picture but that didn't
work. So I asked them, 'Can you pose again for me?'
They did and I took this photo. Such power I have!
The signage on the wall added to the tale.

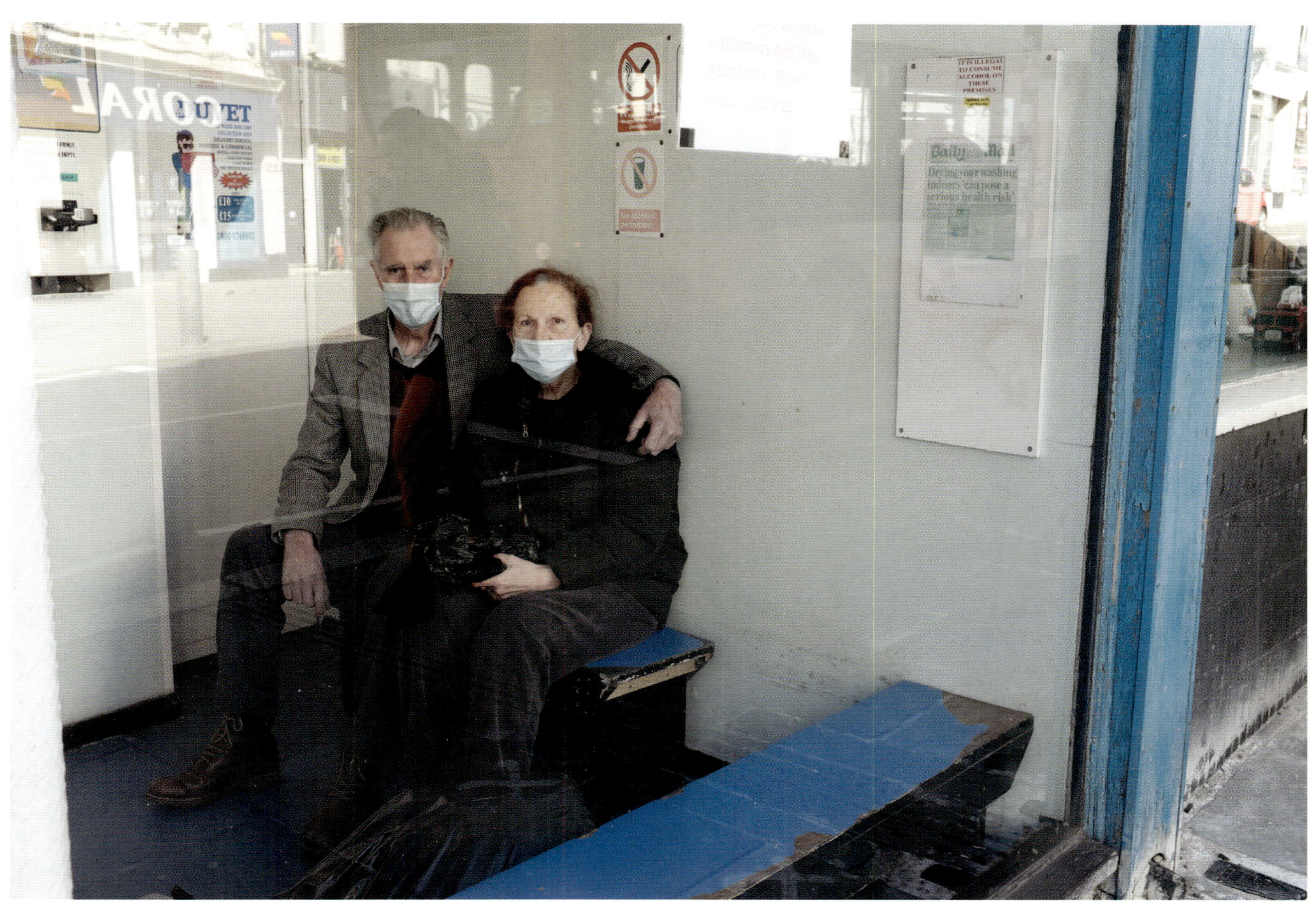
No alcohol permitted
IT IS ILLEGAL
TO CONSUME
ALCOHOL ON
THESE
PREMISES
Daily Mail
Drying your washing
indoors 'can pose a
serious health risk'

Some municipal building.
I just thought it was funny.

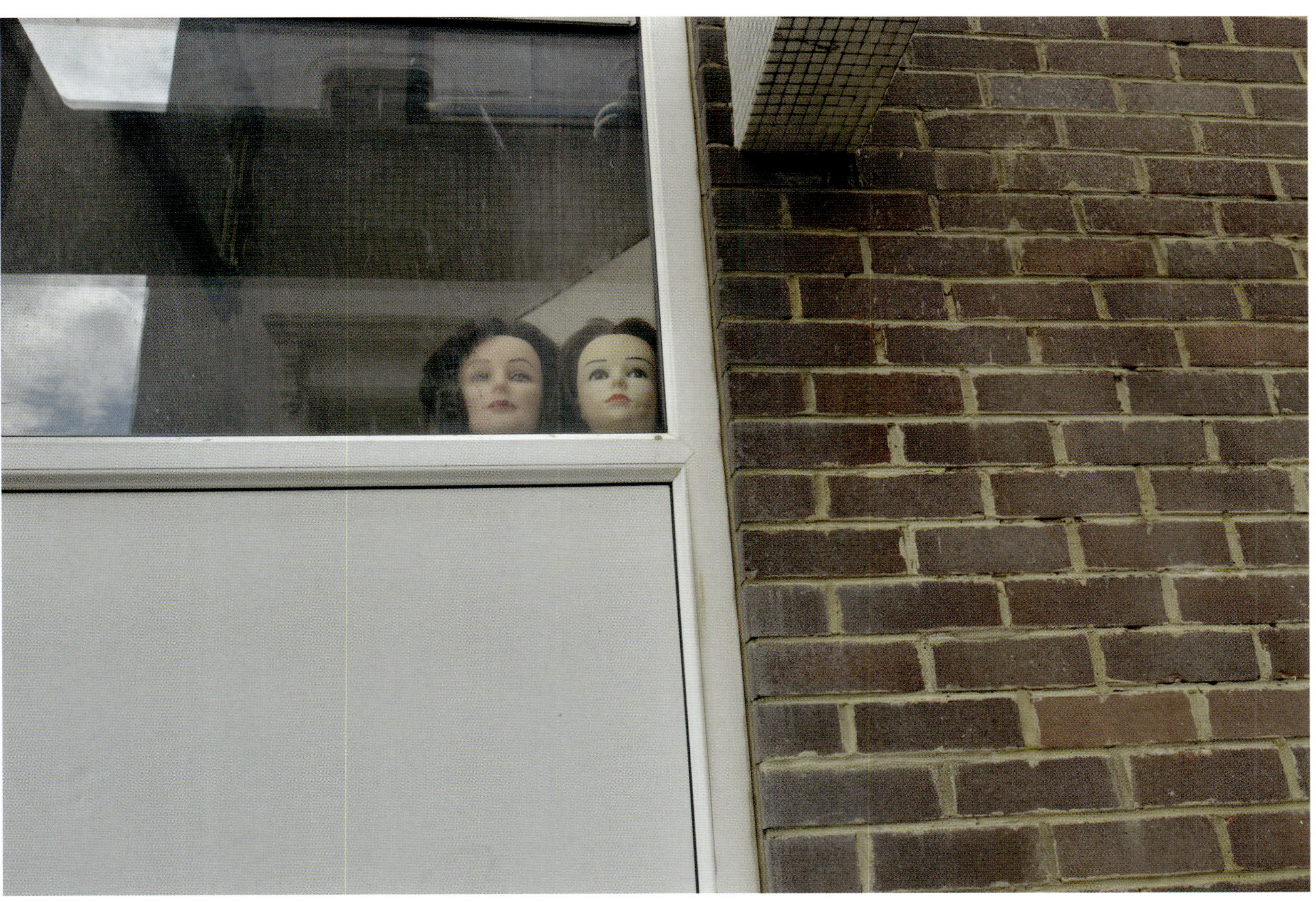

Nick and his dog.

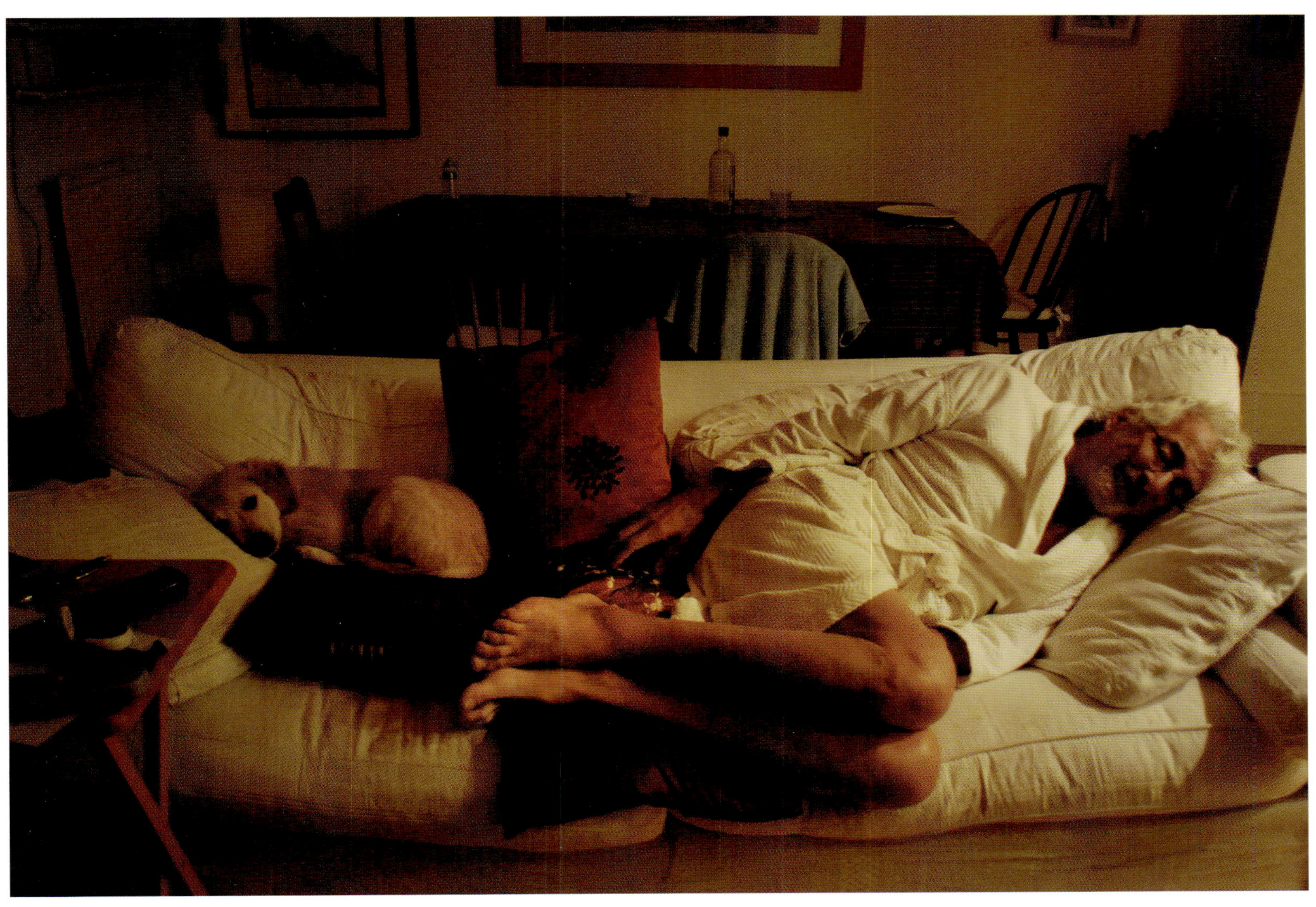

Taken from West Hill looking to the East Hill.
It looks like you're in Nepal. I see those clouds
as mountains behind tiny, little humans.

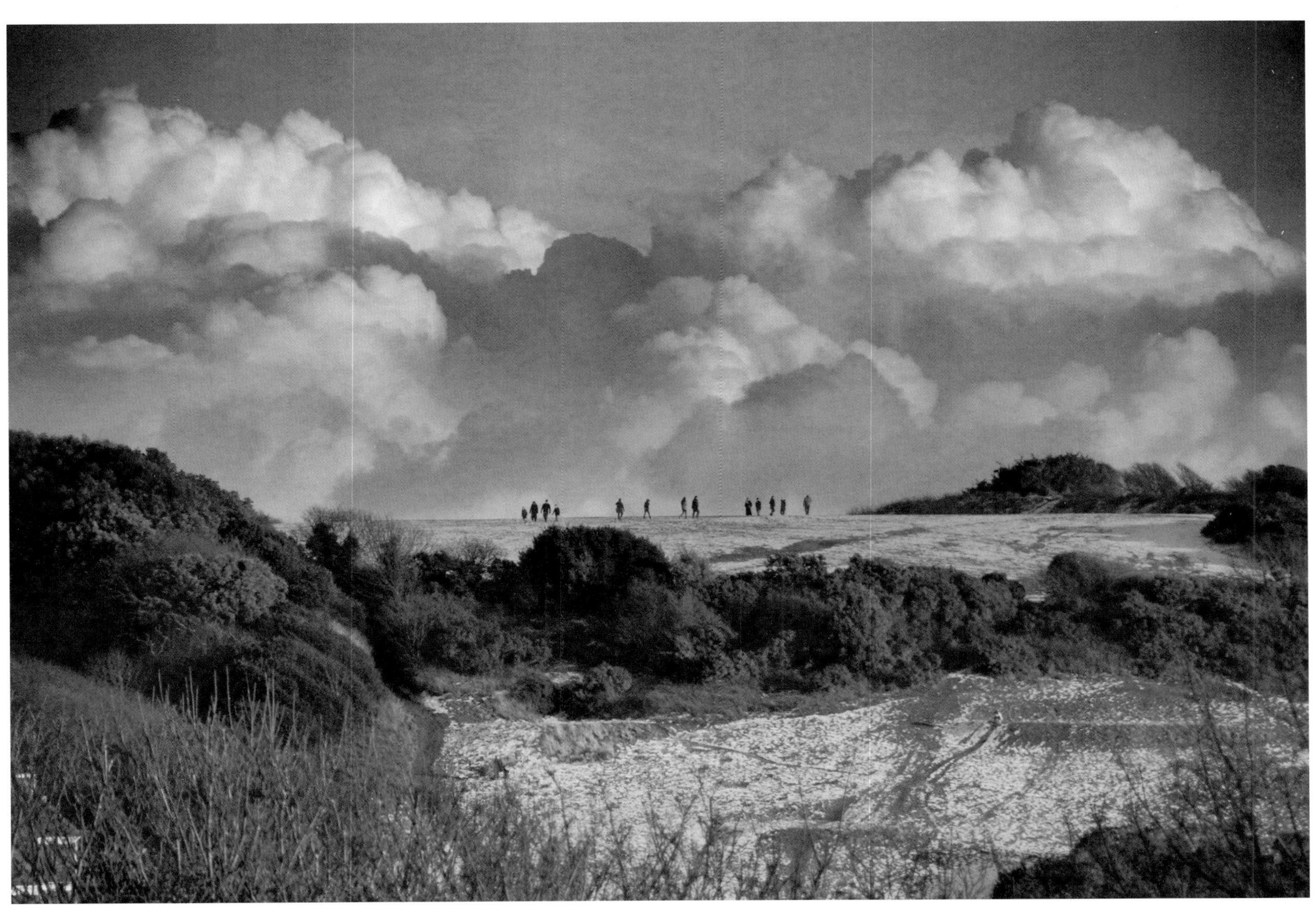

A kids' marching band. Kids doing what they
should be doing rather than playing on screens.

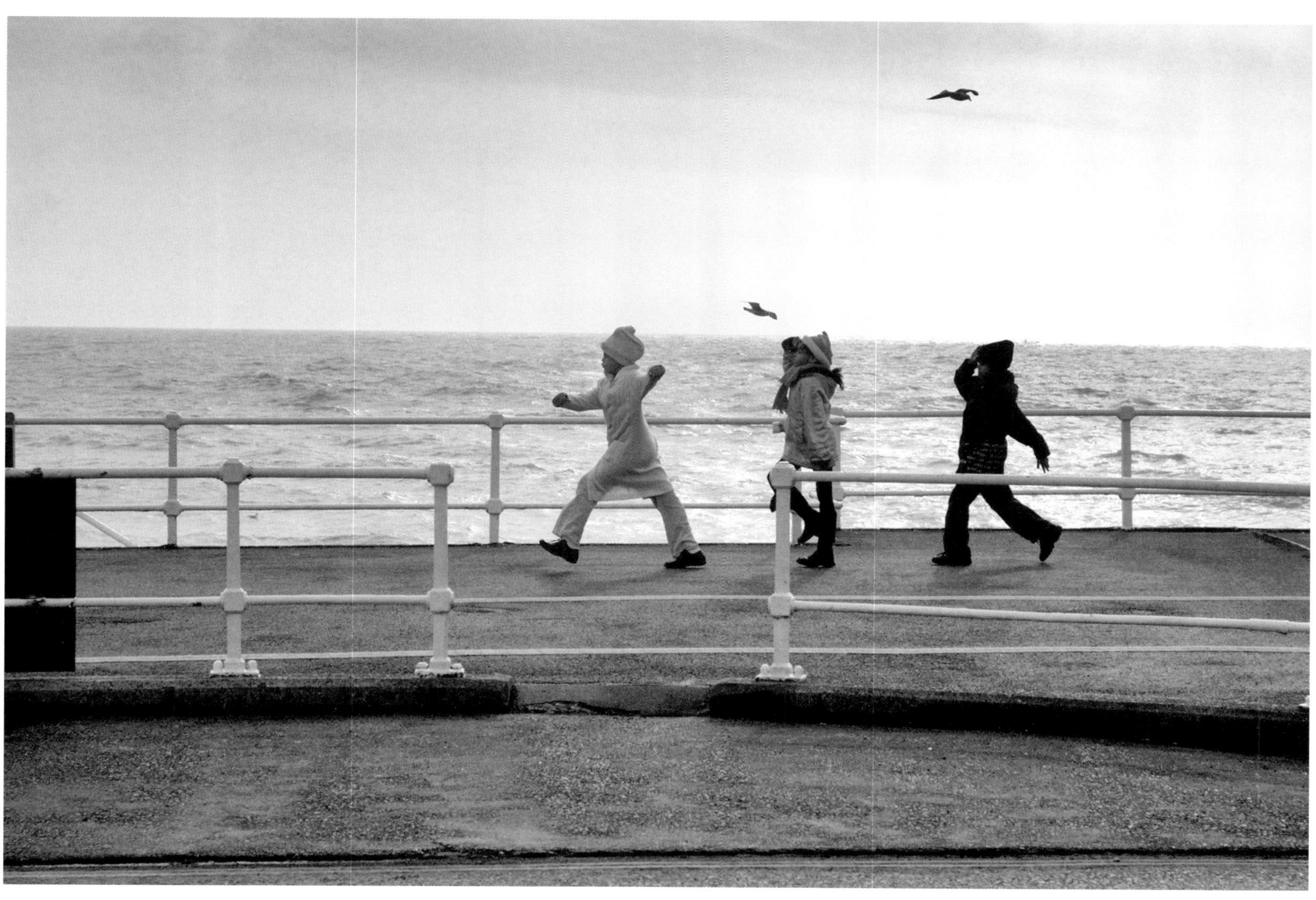

Man with larch. I love this as a portrait. Slightly
meaningful but what it is about, I don't know.
The mystery of larch.

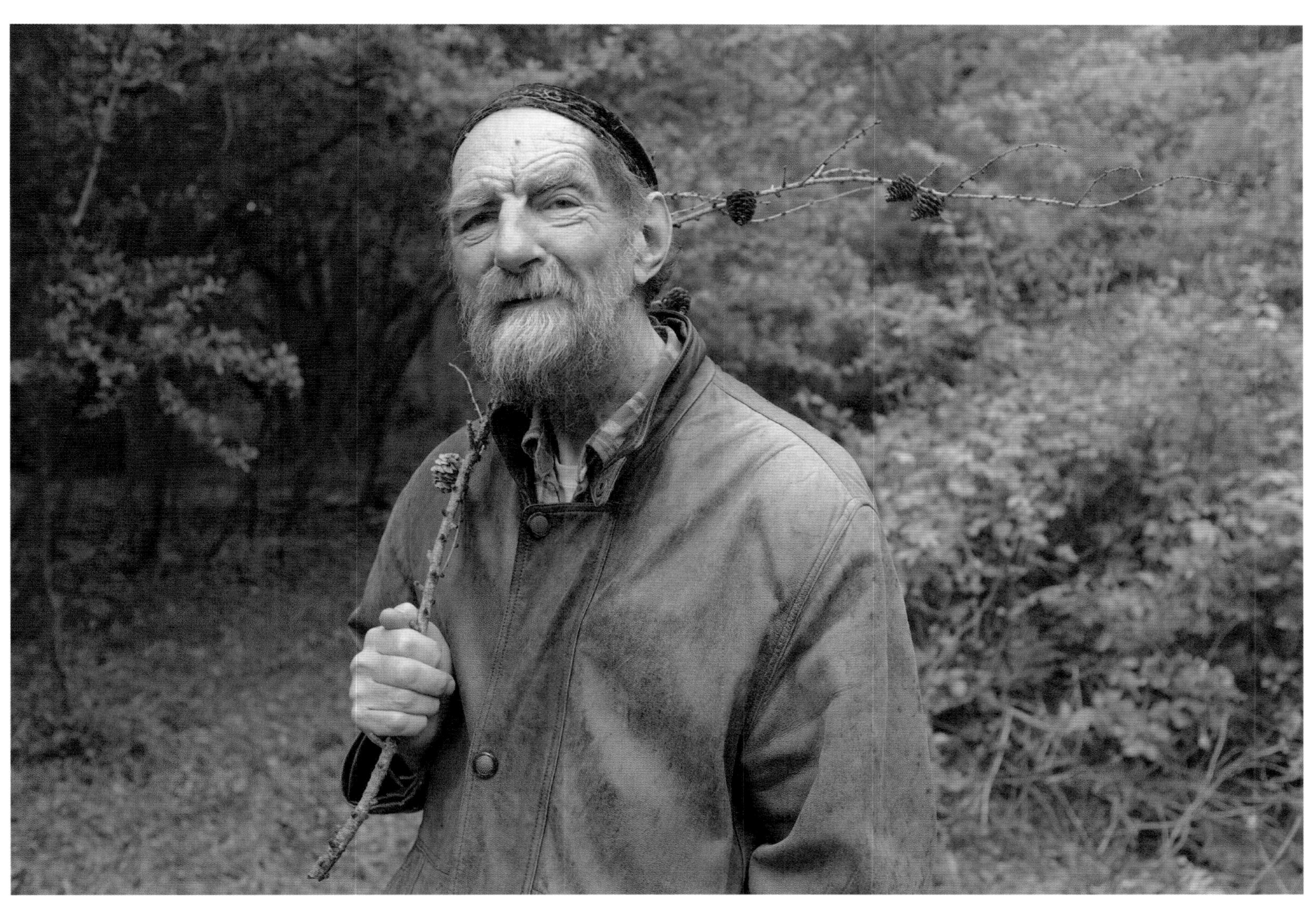

Jack in the Green. Collier Road.

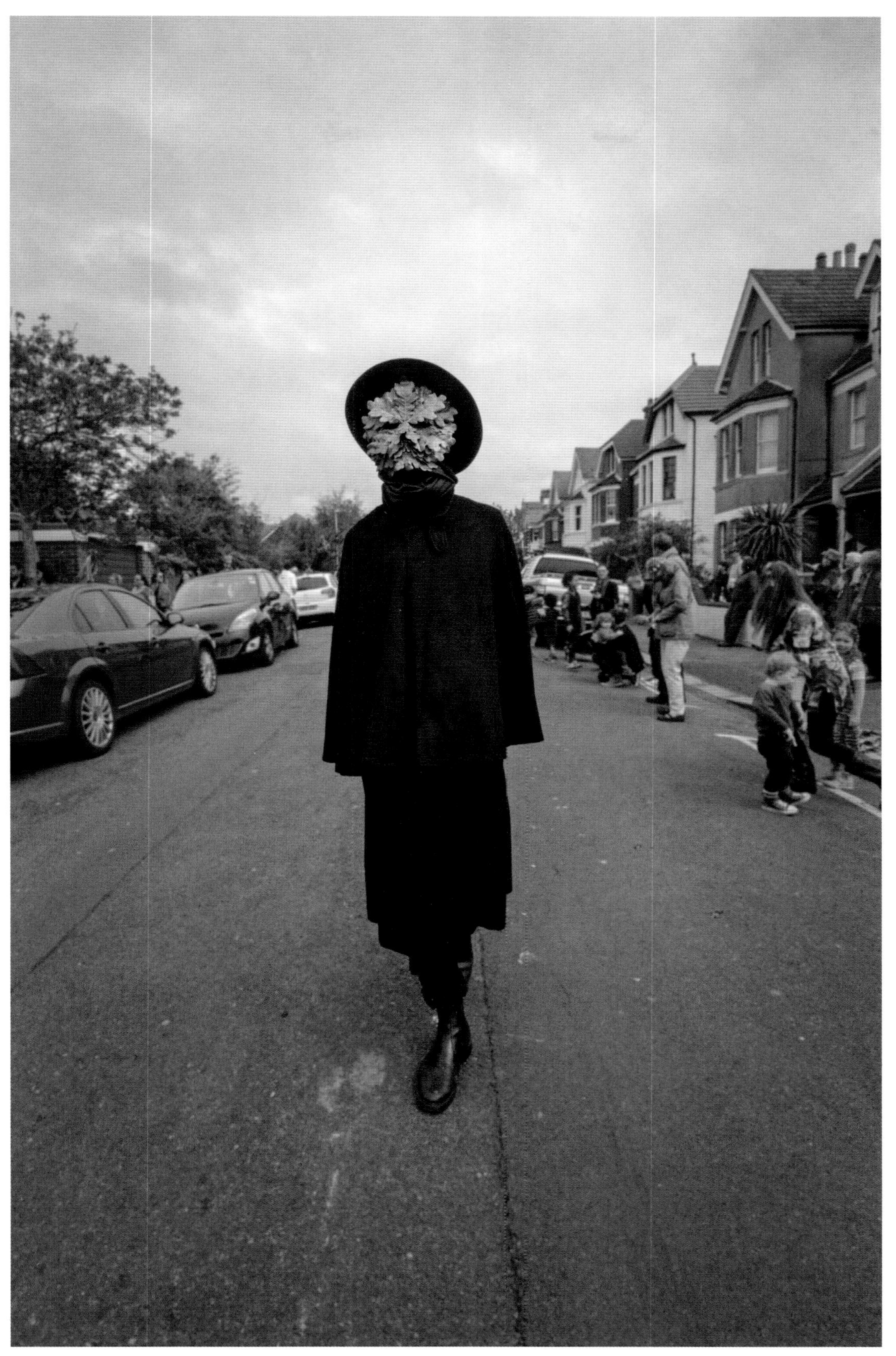

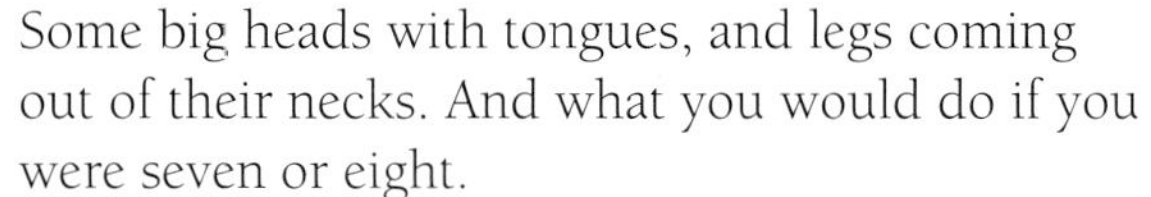
Some big heads with tongues, and legs coming
out of their necks. And what you would do if you
were seven or eight.

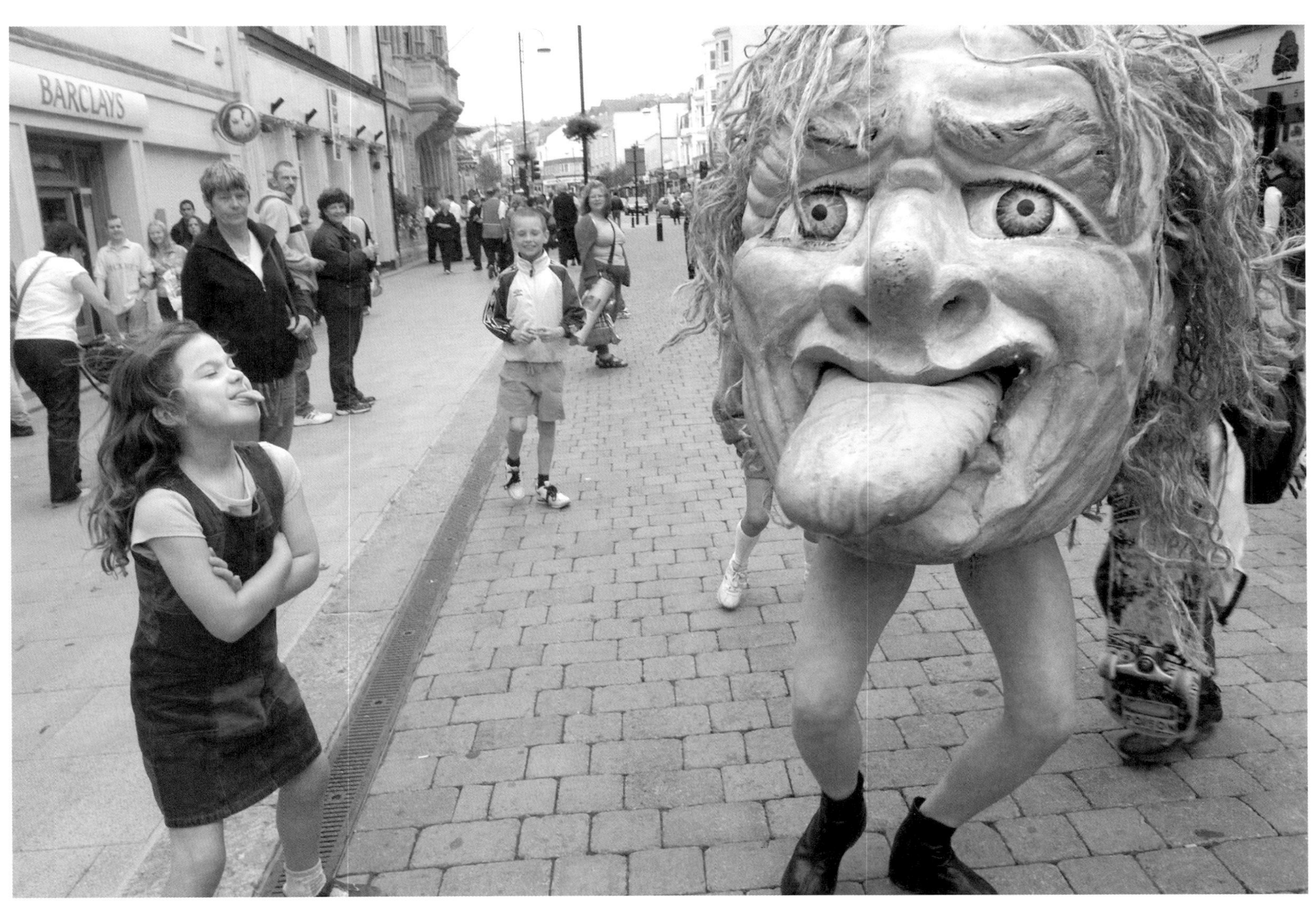

A knickers' shot. If you're going to shoot drive-by, why not? I know I shouldn't feel bad about taking photos of this through the car window, but I don't want to be considered weird.

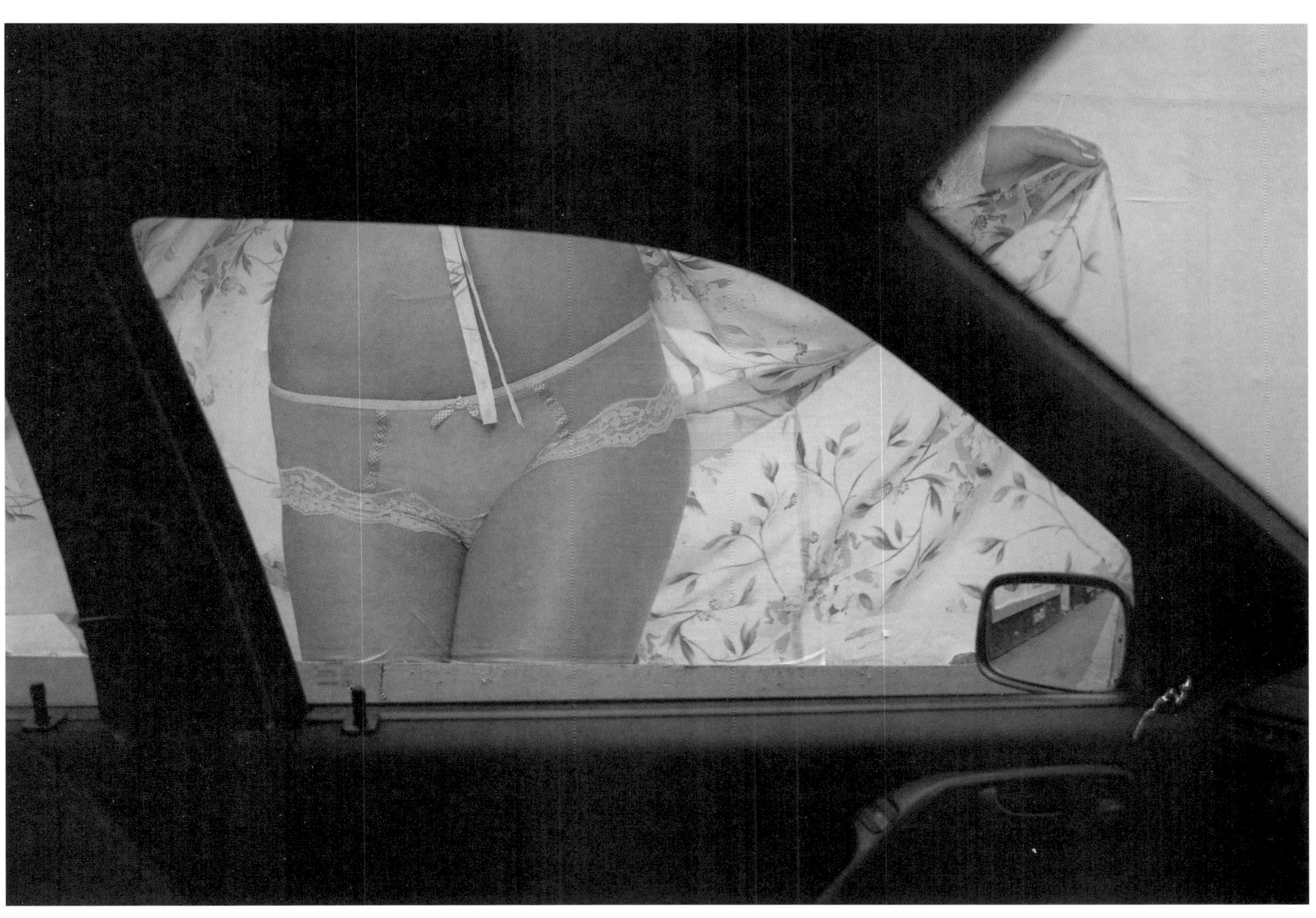

A council job. The inauguration of the Stade space.
A twirling hula hoop artiste. But it's more than
that. I love the look on her face. It does have some
meaning for me.

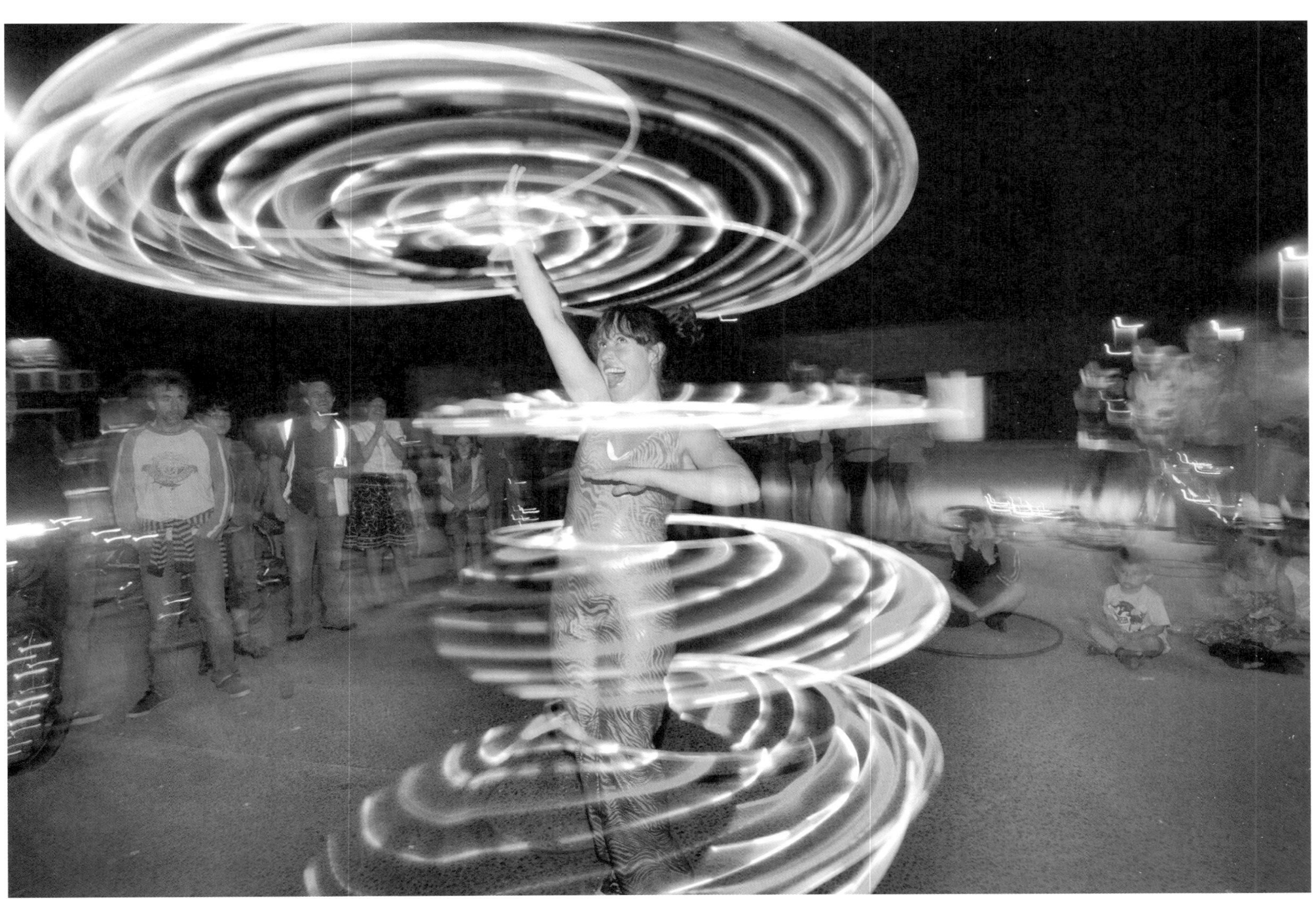

Lovelorn signs.

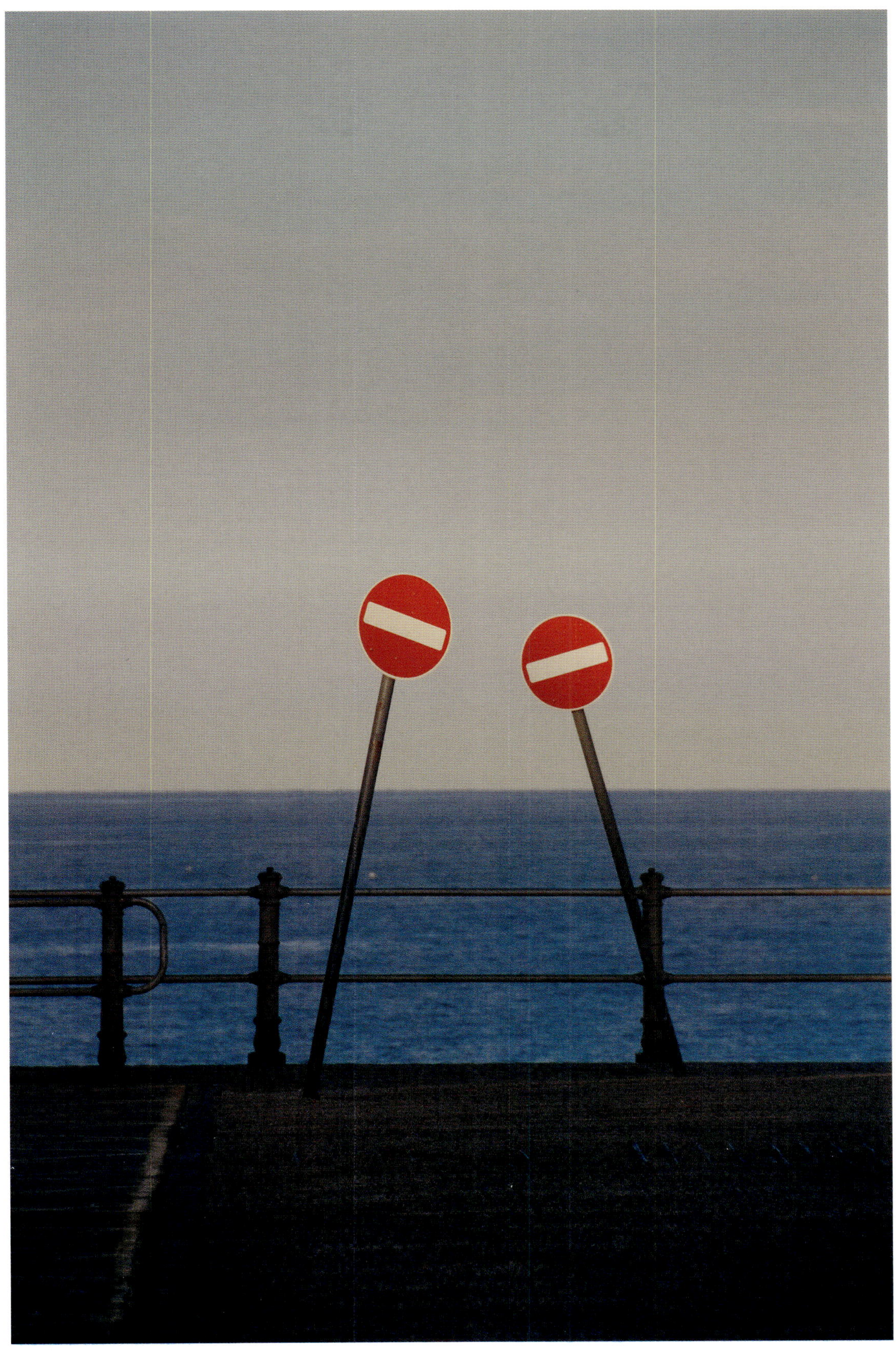

Last light standing.
Makes me think of that Magritte painting. I am in
no way comparing myself to Magritte but it makes
me think of *Empire of Light*.

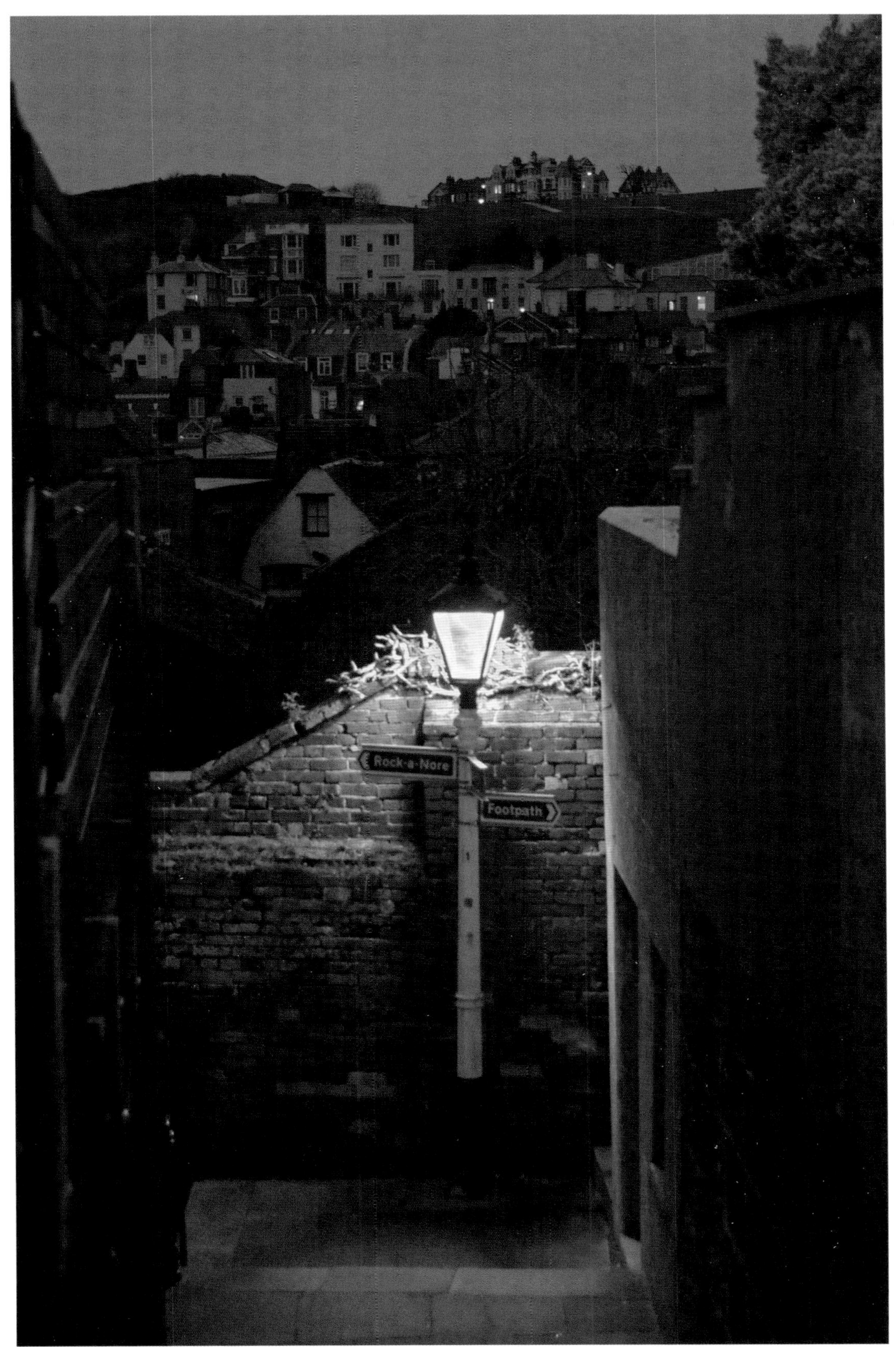

Rock-a-Nore
Footpath

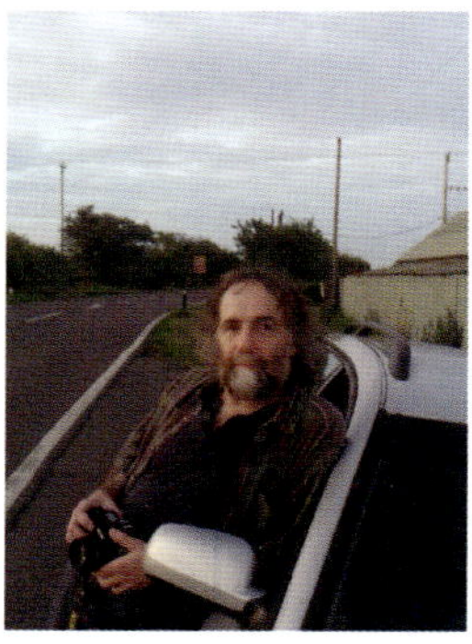

Bob Mazzer attended Hornsey College of Art, under the tutorage of the wonderful Italian photographer, Enzo Ragazzini, and during the eventful years of the late 1960s, enjoyed the freedom and new ideas generated during the famous *Sit In*, a formative element of the counter-culture of the day. As a young photographer he was part of the London scene, worked regularly for *Oz* and *Time Out* magazines and exhibiting at the Photographers' Gallery, the Serpentine Gallery, the Bibliothéque in Paris and photo festivals in Arles and Cologne.

He was born in the East End of London and though he has lived both in and out of the capital (particularly enjoying four years or so in the early-to-mid 1970s, leading a simultaneously tranquil/riotous life in the foothills of Powys, Wales), he has spent the last thirty years living in Hastings with Jen, a painter and illustrator, and their two children, Alice, a biochemical engineer, and Arthur, a sound engineer (now both flown). Bob was given his first camera, an Ilford Sporty – a very basic camera with a rather lovely lens – for his Bar Mitzvah and he fell in love with photography. He took and processed his first photos in 1963 (assisted by the revolutionary decision to build a darkroom in the Art Department of Woodberry Down Comprehensive School and employ Euan Duff, a freelance photographer with a definite socialist bent, who inspired great admiration in Bob by rolling up to teach in a beaten-up green Land Rover and roll neck sweater – what's more, swore in the dark room!).

In 1969, Bob visited the USA, taking what he considered to be his earliest photographs of any significance, and which were published in both *Creative Camera* and *The British Journal of Photography*. His most well-known photographs were taken on the London Underground over a period of forty years, generating a hugely successful exhibition in 2014 and a worldwide interest, with photos appearing in various publications from *National Geographic* to *Professional Photographer*, a Chinese photo magazine with the widest readership in China. In a more recent acknowledgement of the Tube pictures as a unique social document, *Time Out* magazine included Bob's photograph of a bespectacled woman smoking a cigarette on the Tube in its list of forty of the greatest photos of London ever taken.

The photographs shown in this book are the natural result of a photographer interested in his local surroundings and populated by its myriad characters, and are in many ways a family album, showing Bob's love for his own *Family of Man**.

**Family of Man* is a famous book published in the 1950s illustrating the highs and lows of humanity in photos taken by several top reportage and documentary photographers of the time. It was also an exhibition.